IMPLEMENTING TOTAL QUALITY

Joe Cullen
and
Jack Hollingum

IFS (Publications) Ltd, UK
Springer-Verlag
Berlin · Heidelberg · New York
London · Paris · Tokyo

Jack Hollingum
IFS (Publications) Ltd
35–39 High Street
Kempston
Bedford MK42 7BT
England

Joe Cullen
Coopers & Lybrand Associates
Harman House
1 George Street
Uxbridge UB8 1QQ
England

British Library Cataloguing in Publication Data

Cullen, Joe
 Implementing Total Quality
 1. Quality control
 I. Title II. Hollingum, Jack
 658.5'62   TS156

ISBN 0-948507-65-9 IFS (Publications) Ltd
ISBN 3-540-18242-X Springer-Verlag Berlin
ISBN 0-387-18242-X Springer-Verlag New York

© 1987 **IFS (Publications) Ltd,** 35–39 High Street, Kempston,
              Bedford MK42 7BT, UK
  Springer-Verlag Berlin Heidelberg New York
              London Paris Tokyo

Phototypeset by Parchment (Oxford) Ltd
Printed by Bartham Press Ltd, Luton

Foreword

It has been said that there will be two kinds of company in the future – companies which have implemented Total Quality and companies which are out of business.

The majority of chief executives that I meet today admit that they want to do something about the quality of their products and services. Very often they have already isolated some of the tools for quality improvement (e.g. quality circles, quality education, statistical process control), and they are bulldozing them into position in their organisation. Very often, however, these same executives come back six months later and tell me "It didn't work out, the programme failed, we still have a problem with quality." If you approach quality management using isolated tools, regarding it as merely a one-off programme, without being committed to a total cultural change in the organisation, your efforts will be wasted, and the approach will fail.

The purpose of this book on Total Quality is to give you a clear understanding of the management of quality improvement, as well as providing a detailed and structured approach to implementing a programme of Total Quality.

Be warned: it is not an easy route, and there are very few short cuts, but if your business interest is survival, then it is a journey that you must take, and the sooner you embark, the more chance you have to be at the finishing post alongside your competitors.

When I joined the ITT Corporation in 1973, there was a Total Quality system in operation on a worldwide basis. The profit contribution due to quality improvements was significant, and the company's reputation for product and service quality was renowned. In my 13 years with the corporation, we never let up in the quest for continuous quality improvement. Total Quality is still a major goal for ITT, but it is also a way of life.

No one can afford not to consider the advantages of Total Quality. This book is an excellent reference guide for managers in all business sectors. The methodology and the tools are equally applicable to financial institutions and service industries as well as to manufacturing concerns.

Robert M. G. Millar
Director of Quality
Coopers & Lybrand Associates Europe
September 1987

Contents

STRUCTURE

TECHNOLOGY

Joe Cullen has a PhD and a BSc in Mechanical Engineering from Imperial College, London, and an MBA from the University of Glasgow. He is a Chartered Mechanical Engineer and a Member of both the Institution of Mechanical Engineers and the Institute of Quality Assurance. He is the author of several articles on Total Quality, and is currently Manager of Coopers & Lybrand's Total Quality practice in the UK.

Jack Hollingum is a distinguished technical author and journalist, and a former editor of *Sensor Review* magazine. His previous publications include *Machine Vision: The Eyes of Automation* (1984); *The Machine Vision Sourcebook* (1986); and *Implementing an Information Strategy in Manufacture* (1987), all published by IFS.

Preface

We have written this book for two reasons. We are firmly convinced of the importance of Total Quality to today's industry and commerce, and we believe there is a need for an introduction to the subject for senior executives, written in non-specialist language and covering all the essential aspects within one short volume. There are excellent reference works which deal with the subject in depth for specialist quality managers. There are also shorter books on particular topics such as the human aspects of quality, quality circles and statistical process control. It is our contention, though, that a Total Quality policy must pay equally close attention to the human, the structural and the technological aspects, and that neglect of any one of these areas will result in a deficient quality system.

The book is intended to be a practical guide to action on Total Quality, and at the end of every chapter we suggest immediate steps that can be taken towards implementing Total Quality in your company. Included in the book is a flowchart which you can remove and use to monitor the progress of your Total Quality implementation.

A book such as this draws on the experience of many people besides the authors, but we should particularly like to thank those people who gave us information and help in the case studies of Chapter 1 – Alan Ladd of Rank Xerox, Dr T. J. Vickerstaff of Jaguar Cars, Michael Chupa of ITT Hancock Industries, Stewart McCausland of Electrolux, and Frank Scanlon of Hartford Insurance Group. For the excellent example in Chapter 9 of supplier collaboration in the food manufacturing industry we are indebted to Steve Eastham of Coopers & Lybrand.

Bob Millar, director of quality, Coopers & Lybrand Europe, read the manuscript in detail, and we are thankful to him for many helpful comments – though the responsibility for any remaining defects is ours. Finally our long-suffering wives, with many responsibilities of their own, have had to carry an undue share of family duties, and it is only because of their support that this book has been possible – our grateful thanks to them.

1 SUCCESS STORIES

Total Quality means zero defects and reduced product costs

Total Quality means exactly what it says – zero defects in products leaving the factory and in services offered. It means quality in every aspect of the company's operations. It also means more than it says. You might think that the achievement of near-perfection in quality would involve a cost penalty for the company. The reverse is true. The costs incurred in implementing Total Quality are far outweighed by the savings it produces, both directly, in terms of the elimination of wasted time, effort and materials throughout the company, and in enhanced business resulting from greater competitiveness and better customer relations.

To whet your appetite for Total Quality, and to show

that it is a practical and extremely worthwhile policy for any organisation, we begin this book with a few examples of the results which are being achieved by companies which have committed themselves to a policy of Total Quality. We have selected cases from widely differing business sectors to underline the fact that Total Quality is not only a philosophy for manufacturing companies, but can transform the operation of any organisation in industry, commerce or public service. All of the companies have an exciting story to tell, but we have selected one of them – Rank Xerox – for a more extended description of the process which helped the company recover from near-disaster to hold its own in a fiercely competitive market.

Top management must make a firm and sustained commitment to Total Quality

All of the examples have a great deal in common, despite the wide differences between the companies and their products. In every case, though, one requirement stands out as more important than any other: *there must be a firm and sustained commitment to Total Quality from the top of the organisation downwards.*

RANK XEROX

Rank Xerox is a company which, along with its parent Xerox Corporation, has experienced traumatic losses and cuts in its scale of operation as a result of Japanese competition, combined with an approaching saturation in the market for plain-paper copiers, which have been the company's staple product. After growing at 30% annually through the early 1970s and reaching a record pre-tax profit of £316 million in 1977, with a turnover of nearly £1,000 million, the company held its own for a couple more years. Then profits fell dramatically every year, until in 1983 they were down to £166 million. Since then, Rank Xerox has been fighting its way back, with profits growth averaging about 10% annually and the realistic expectation of a similar revenue growth rate over the next few years.

The company attributes its success in arresting and reversing its catastrophic decline to one thing: a quality improvement programme which has completely transformed the way the whole company thinks and works. The results of the programme are typified by the graph in Fig. 1.1. This shows how the number of defects has fallen at the company's Mitcheldean plant, the principal Xerox manufacturing unit in Europe. To measure overall product quality, Rank Xerox has developed a composite index based on all the products manufactured at Mitcheldean. Each product has a number of drawings associated with it – many thousands in the case of the large copying machines and electronic printers, some 2,000 for the small desktop copiers. The overall index of defects is calculated as a certain number of defects per thousand drawings, including all the company's manufactured products.

As the graph shows, the defect index fell dramatically almost from the beginning of the quality improvement programme. The achievement was so impressive that at the end of 1984 the company won the British Quality Award. The rate of improvement started to level off in 1985, and Rank Xerox is now engaged in a new phase of the

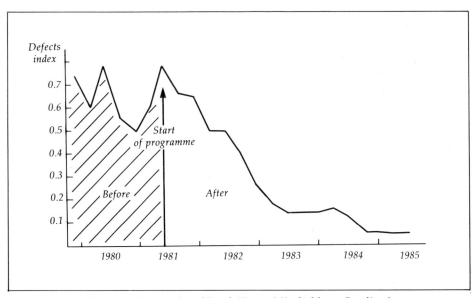

Fig. 1.1. Product quality results of Rank Xerox Mitcheldean Quality Improvement Programme

programme, involving not only activities from engineering through to production and dispatch but the whole business, including finance, sales and personnel, with the aim of reducing defects still further.

The Rank Xerox policy on quality improvement is very similar to the approach we shall be proposing in this book. It includes three key statements:

● Quality is the fundamental business principle.
● Internal as well as external customers must be satisfied.
● Quality improvement is the job of every employee.

A steering committee coordinates the quality programme

The company adopted competitive benchmarking to set its future goals, aiming to be better than the best, and setting up a three- to five-year implementation programme. From the beginning, and still today, the programme has been implemented from the top. At Mitcheldean it is managed by a steering committee chaired by the plant director and consisting of direct reporting managers. Quality is not delegated. The committee is responsible for coordinating the quality improvement process through all the plant functions. Its objectives are:

● To improve customer satisfaction.
● To increase competitiveness.
● To reduce the cost of quality.

'Quality' is defined by Rank Xerox as full conformance to agreed customer requirements, and the 'customer' is defined as not only the buyer of the company's products, but as everybody, inside or outside the company, who is at the receiving end of materials, services or information. The production scheduling department, for example, is a customer of sales order processing, and process planning is a customer of product design.

From this definition it can be seen that it is important to know exactly who one's customers are and what their requirements are, and to reach an agreement with the customers about those requirements. The result of this process is an agreed specification. Quality embraces continuing conformance to the specification at an acceptable cost and delivery.

Five areas were identified as crucial to the improvement of quality:

- Product design.
- Material conformance.
- Production processes.
- Business support.
- Awareness and training.

Project teams follow through the crucial issues

Projects were identified in these areas, and many teams worked simultaneously to bring about changes. In product design, projects included the improvement of product and parts specifications to avoid ambiguity, an analysis of quality-critical parts to ensure that the design minimises production problems, and the introduction of a number of steps to help the production operator achieve improved quality and consistency.

Analysis of suppliers by material conformance teams showed that most of the non-conforming parts were being produced by just a few suppliers. A team from Mitcheldean therefore visited each of them, starting at the worst, and presented them with a training programme on quality improvement. Each supplier's production process was evaluated by the Rank Xerox Supplier Quality Assurance Engineer, and statistical process control established for all critical parts. A scheme of certification for good-quality incoming parts was set up, allowing conforming parts to pass straight to assembly without goods inward inspection.

Study of the requirements for improvement of production processes led to the introduction of in-process controls with immediate feedback to the operator responsible for the work, so that the process could be maintained under control. This change required the use of control charts by operators. In addition, a weekly quality workshop was introduced, led by the supervisor, where problem-solving techniques could be applied to the more difficult problems. A system of operator 'qualification' was adopted for operators who could demonstrate their ability to maintain a certain quality standard.

Business support is an aspect of the quality improvement programme which is now gaining much more attention as the more obvious design and production areas have been brought under better control. For example, if the accounts department allows invoices to become overdue, suppliers may not deliver parts on time, with serious consequences for assembly.

Training was seen by Rank Xerox to be an essential element in developing the quality improvement process throughout the company. There has been a comprehensive training activity since the beginning of the quality improvement programme, starting with the senior executives and continuing into middle management. All the managers were asked to define their outputs and their 'customers' in the previously discussed sense of the word. They were then expected to work on the strategic problems of meeting their customers' needs.

Training is continued through 'family groups'

The training activity has continued through the company to all levels, and at every level both the training and the subsequent quality improvement activity have taken place in what are called 'family groups', comprising a peer group of employees, together with their supervisor, who is responsible for their training. The members of a management group first absorb the new way of thinking and get to grips with defining their outputs and the cost of failing to meet their customers' needs. Then it is the turn of each of them to teach their subordinates within their family groups. In this way, the understanding and application of the quality improvement policy has percolated downward, albeit rather slowly, until by now every employee has been through the training programme.

Each family group measures its performance in terms of a number of key outputs, such as drawings issued, tools produced or parts kitted, chosen to give an indication of customer satisfaction; and these quantities are monitored to give the group an indication of its progress against a target which it has set in cooperation with its 'customers'. To deal with specific problems, the groups form project teams, led by a member of the group. A team may if necessary co-opt suppliers and customers to help solve its problem and raise its quality to the target level or beyond. Each month, as project teams propose new ideas for raising quality, a 'top team' is selected, which is awarded a prize of £250 to be donated to a charity of the team's choice.

A 'Quality Convention' adds incentive – and supports charity

Once a year, there is a 'Quality Convention' at Mitcheldean, at which the year's top teams make a presentation of the results of their work. Prior to the convention, a secret evaluation is made of their work, and at the convention the winning top team for the year is announced. The winning team gets an additional £1,000 for charity, and presentations are made at the convention to representatives of all the charities which have been nominated. The quality conventions have proved to be a strong motivator for the project teams, which often come back for a second year to try and beat their previous record. They also support the publicity programme aimed at developing and maintaining awareness throughout the company of the importance of quality improvement.

An indication of the scope of activities of the project teams is given by the subjects covered by some of the top teams at the 1986 Quality Convention. These included: an international project to reduce freight costs; reducing the frequency of paper jamming on one type of copying machine, making possible nearly £3 million savings over the product life; improving the working environment in a subassembly section; improving the reliability of a pallet conveyor, saving £15,000 a year and avoiding the need for replacement at a cost of £100,000; improving the production of data on outlooks for material inventories, labour overheads and other information, resulting in data becoming available two days earlier and saving one day for input; and an analysis of the lack of communication between departments in one part of the business and the implementation of a number of steps to improve it.

JAGUAR CARS

The transformation of Jaguar Cars has become a legend during the few years in which it has taken place. Jaguar was originally a company with a very high reputation, but by the time John Egan, the current chairman, took over in

1980, the company's reputation for quality had sunk to a low ebb, even though the vehicle design was still excellent. Markets were disintegrating, long-term Jaguar owners were having their loyalty tested beyond endurance, and the company was given only months to live.

Now, only seven years later, the reputation of the company is second to none. In 1980 Jaguar built 13,500 cars with 14,000 people. In 1986 it built 40,000 cars with 10,000 people. Productivity has trebled in the past five years, turnover has increased enormously, and profits for 1986 amounted to £120 million.

A survey of customers reveals opportunities for improvement

The root cause of Jaguar's troubles was quality. A report at the time described the Series III saloon as 'a magnificent world class car failing to realise its true sales potential due to poor and inconsistent quality, and the rapid acquisition of a reputation for unreliability'. Quality and reliability were therefore made the first priority of the company. Hundreds of Jaguar owners were asked questions about their vehicles, and the results of that survey, together with warranty data, revealed the scale of the problems to be overcome. The whole company was reorientated around the urgent need to deal with the faults which were revealed. Multidisciplinary task forces were set up to deal with the major faults, and, where appropriate, the teams included representatives of Jaguar's suppliers. It was brought home to everybody in the company that quality was their business, and the phrase 'in pursuit of perfection' was coined, both as an internal slogan and for use in an advertising campaign.

Dr T. J. Vickerstaff, Jaguar's manager of current production engineering, points out that the word 'pursuit' implies a chase after something that is trying to get away. Quality is not a goal which, once reached, can be sustained without constant effort. The 'goalposts' are always moving. Competitors improve, suppliers slip, customer demands change and increase. So Jaguar's future plans are to achieve further growth while not only maintaining its hard-won quality but also improving standards even further.

ITT HANCOCK INDUSTRIES

The Automotive Electrical Division of the ITT Hancock Industries Group introduced Total Quality at its plant in Matamoros, Mexico, early in 1984. This was at a time when the Division had been losing business from major customers because of poor quality and late delivery. The system of Process Control, as it was called, is outlined in Fig. 1.2. It defines management's and workers' responsibility for improving performance.

The philosophy of Total Quality was readily adopted at Matamoros, and gains were rapid and dramatic – so much so that by 1985 there had been a 70% reduction in total quality costs, a 79% decrease in scrap, and an 85% decrease in appraisal costs as compared with 1983. Fig. 1.3 shows how the percentage of defectives at final audit fell during this period, and Fig. 1.4 indicates the effect on the plant's productivity percentage.

Dramatic improvements can be obtained through better product development

The area offering the greatest return for effort expended was, as we shall show in this book, product development. Through team participation during the early stages of new product life, the rate of acceptance by customers of samples submitted rose from 84% to 98%, and these efforts helped to alleviate the subsequent unevenness in productivity and quality during manufacturing startup.

A programme of statistical process control was introduced through seminars for each level of workers in the company. This helped in controlling key process parameters and was used to monitor improvements. Assembly defects were substantially cut as a result of giving operators the responsibility and authority to stop a line when a defect occurred. The Taguchi method for design of experiments (see Chapter 12) was also introduced and resulted in major improvements in welding and other processes. As a result of its performance on quality, the Matamoros plant won the Ford Motor Company Q-1 award in 1985, and the ITT Silver Bowl in 1986.

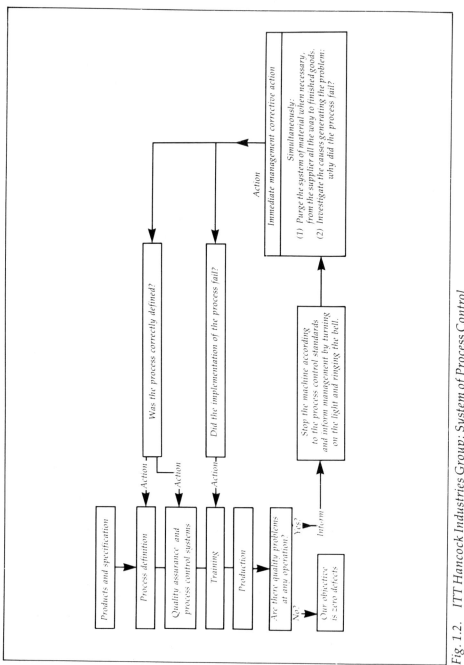

Fig. 1.2.   ITT Hancock Industries Group: System of Process Control

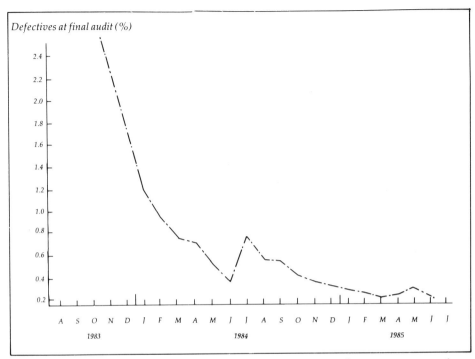

Defectives at final audit (%)

Fig. 1.3. Total Quality implementation at ITT's Matamoros plant – percentage of defectives at final audit

ELECTROLUX

In 1982 the 15 European manufacturing plants of this world-class domestic appliance manufacturer were astonished to receive a decree from their group chief executive to the effect that they were to reduce their warranty failure levels by 50% by the end of 1984. Early in 1985 they were told that they would have to reduce warranty failures by a further 50% by the end of 1987 – effectively amounting to a 75% reduction in the space of five years.

Stewart McCausland, quality engineer at the company's plant in Luton, UK, shared with a recent conference the thought that ironically, because people in industry generally have been talking about quality, and top managements have been 'supporting' the idea of quality for

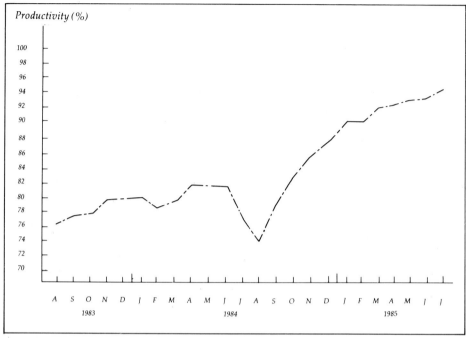

Fig. 1.4.   Total Quality implementation at ITT's Matamoros plant – effect on productivity percentage

so many years, and so many panaceas have been offered, people have become 'punch-drunk' and have actually ended by doing very little about it. In the case of Electrolux it took the total commitment of the person at the top of the group and a clearly defined objective to achieve a real impact.

Electrolux was not in anything like the desperate situation that Jaguar had faced in 1980. There were no obvious deficiencies in Electrolux products. The company already had what it considered to be a high consumer awareness for quality. The chief executive's action had been provoked by the realisation that if the company were to continue to succeed as one of the world's top domestic appliance manufacturers, its quality would have to be as good, if not better, than its competitors'. This meant achieving levels of quality comparable to those of Japanese companies.

At the beginning of the campaign in 1982, the Luton service department had virtually completed a computerised system for all customer service calls under warranty, so the company had very accurate and detailed data on field failure levels and therefore knew how extensive a task lay ahead. However, it was determined to achieve its objective, and monitored progress on a monthly basis.

The initial results were disappointing, and as time went by they became more disturbing. When 12 months had passed with no real breakthrough – in fact the position had deteriorated – it was obvious that something was badly amiss. With the benefit of hindsight, according to McCausland, it is easy to explain why the early expectations were not fulfilled. The efforts were concentrated on applying to quality much the same approach as before, albeit in a more rigorous way. Thus every manager inevitably still had a number of objectives, of which only one concerned quality. It was clear that the traditional approach, even with intensified efforts, was insufficient.

Quality must become the first objective for all managers

It was therefore obvious that a radical review of the quality strategy was essential, and once this fundamental reasoning was accepted, the turning-point was reached. Overnight, quality became the first objective for all managers. 'Quality at any price' became the catch-phrase. Reliability testing and auditing of products were implemented on an unprecedented level. Statistical process control for defect prevention became one of the corner-stones of the revised strategy.

The new strategy had its effect. The Luton plant met its first target, and by mid-1987 had all but met its current one; and other manufacturing plants in Europe and Scandinavia are now coming to Luton for advice and training, particularly in the use of statistical process control.

THE HARTFORD INSURANCE GROUP

It would be hard to find a better example of Total Quality in the service industries than the Hartford Insurance Group

Quality improvement is equally effective in commerce

– a 20,000-strong organisation based in Hartford, Connecticut, with offices in about 60 major locations. Ten years ago it was considered by its insurance agents to be one of the least desirable companies to do business with. Today it is rated the best. In 1976, according to Frank Scanlon, the company's director of quality and education, it had a measured invalid data rate of 40%. For the past three years this has been running at less than 3%. It is not only improved quality that has resulted from the company's programme – there is documented proof of savings amounting to more than $7 million a year, and the actual total is probably more.

The Hartford Insurance quality improvement programme is quite a venerable institution compared with most: it has been running for 11 years. It began with a pre-implementation phase involving analysis of the work process and elimination of unnecessary work – much as would be done in a manufacturing company. Tasks were combined and streamlined, and where appropriate they were automated. Checks were built in to ensure that faults were detected as early as possible, since not only are these less costly when they are detected quickly, but there is also greater educational benefit in helping to avoid their repetition.

The implementation steps in the quality control process for a service company are much the same as for a manufacturing company. At Hartford the process began with obtaining the commitment of all the company executives and securing their leadership in the training programme throughout the company. Quality is the responsibility of line management; there is a corporate quality department, but it has only four members and its primary responsibility is the training of managers to fulfil their quality responsibilities. The department is also responsible for the development of quality systems.

It might be thought that detailed measurement would be a prerogative of manufacturing operations, but Hartford lays great stress on the importance of sampling to locate the sources of errors; checking the results of sampling against written standards; recording all errors, regardless of source; analysing the results and identifying the major problems; taking corrective action and integrating people into the quality cycle; and verifying the results through follow-up audits to ensure that the steps taken were the correct ones and had the desired effect. These stages describe the problem-solving cycle which would be appropriate for any company in any industry.

A special feature of the Hartford programme is its emphasis on communications, and particularly on recognition of its people's contributions to quality. As Scanlon puts it to the company's managers: "98% of our people do their job well all the time – tell them that you appreciate their achievement". There is also stress on communication up the hierarchy and between departments. The company runs an improvement proposals system through which people can make proposals or ask questions about improvements in productivity or quality. The system is very popular, attracting about 3,000 proposals annually.

ACTION SUMMARY

This book is intended to lead to greater business effectiveness as a result of commitment to Total Quality. At the end of each chapter we shall propose an 'Action Summary' comprising certain steps which you can take immediately to discover the present state of your company and to implement a strategy for continuous quality improvement. At the end of the book, Chapter 13 outlines a programme for implementing Total Quality.

2 THE TASK

Make it right the first time, every time

This book is about profitability, and how you can improve it by the implementation of Total Quality. Profitability is stressed because quality has in the past been chained to the ideas of inspection and of costly hindrances to productivity. However, Total Quality, if it is introduced and managed correctly, will:

- Eliminate waste.
- Cut inventories.
- Improve customer satisfaction.
- Enhance profitability.

The case examples given in Chapter 1 are typical of what can be achieved with a well-managed Total Quality programme. They are not unique. Many similar cases, in Britain, Europe, the USA, and particularly in Japan, could have been quoted. The Japanese have adopted the principles of Total Quality with a thoroughness which has contributed strongly to the success of that country's industry in world markets.

At the heart of Total Quality are two simple aims. The first is to *make things right first time*. Nobody tries to make things wrong first time, but Total Quality gives the objective of getting things right the top priority, and uses powerful tools to ensure that it is achieved. The result is the sort of gains reported in Chapter 1.

The second aim is to *work for continual improvement*. Never be satisfied with products or services as they are – they can always be improved. Just think what that means:

● The customer gets something which he or she can brag about so that friends and colleagues want it too.
● No more warranty claims, no failures in service.
● No waste in manufacturing – no scrap, no expensive reworking of defective components or assemblies.
● No consequent disruptions to manufacturing schedules, delayed deliveries, inflated inventories and work in progress.

Few companies realise how great are the costs they are incurring as a result of quality which is less than perfect; they cannot even measure the true cost of defective work. Later in this book you can find out how to measure the cost of inadequate quality in your company. The expense of unsatisfactory quality is most noticeable at the manufacturing end of the company, in scrap, rectification costs and inspection costs. At worst, it results in goods returned from customers and loss of business. The causes of these costs, however, are usually found elsewhere – in wrong marketing decisions, in design weaknesses, in unsatisfactory supplier relations, in plant which is unable to maintain consistent performance. This is another reason why we talk about *Total* Quality. To achieve quality products you must have the involvement of every part of the company.

So far we have discussed Total Quality in manufacturing, but it is equally important in non-manufacturing companies – for example, in distribution, commerce and so on – as will be shown.

THE MEANING OF QUALITY

There is little point in talking about improving quality unless we have a clear idea of what we mean by it. There is more significance and subtlety in the word than might at first be thought.

In popular use, the word suggests a degree of excellence – a Cartier watch, a Rolls-Royce car, a Christian Dior dress: something expensive and conforming to a high, perhaps luxurious, specification. However, this is too imprecise and limited an idea of quality to be of any use in determining company policy.

Quality is fitness for purpose – but what does that mean?

One commonly used definition of quality which originated with one of the pioneers of quality control, Dr J. M. Juran, uses the idea of *fitness for purpose*. Take the case of a Jaguar car. There are several purposes for which it might be bought, of which providing a means of transport is only one, and one that you would expect of any car. One of the most important purposes of a Jaguar (or any other luxury car) is to impress other people. For somebody running a business, for example, a Jaguar is intended to convey the message that the business is successful and profitable. The car needs to be quiet, comfortable, luxurious and relatively spacious, so that clients feel that they are being treated as important people. It needs to create an impression of reliability and speed, suggesting that its owner's business is also reliable and prompt in dealing with its customers.

The reasons for buying a Ford Fiesta will probably be very different. Without wishing to imply anything other than the highest praise for Ford, the main purpose of a Fiesta is to provide low-cost, reliable transport. In some circumstances it might impress the neighbours, but that is not usually a major reason for buying a Fiesta. It needs to be reasonably comfortable, reasonably quiet, not too expensive to buy, inexpensive to run and maintain, and reliable.

Using the 'fitness for purpose' definition of quality, it would be quite possible for the Fiesta to have a higher quality rating than the Jaguar. In fact, Jaguar Cars itself acknowledges that, in these terms, a few years ago it had a bad reputation for quality, whereas Ford has for a long time had a very good reputation in terms of fitness for purpose.

The difficulty about fitness for purpose as a definition is that it is not very helpful in a practical situation. You can't use it to decide whether a car coming off the end of the assembly line has satisfactory quality. Take an example from the other end of the factory – a consignment of tachometers arriving in the goods receiving dock. How do you decide if they are fit for purpose? You can inspect them to see if they are damaged. You can test their performance. Suppose one tachometer is found to read 3% slow. Is that fit for purpose? If it reads 60% slow there is little doubt about its fitness, but something more precise than fitness for purpose is needed as a test for more marginal conditions. There is also the question of who should decide whether an item is fit for purpose: the person receiving the incoming goods? Suppose the next batch is booked in by somebody else with different ideas of fitness for purpose?

Conformance to specification or reliability as a test of quality

All this nebulosity leads to the idea of *conformance to specification* as a test for quality. In fact, the two approaches are not incompatible. At some time someone must draw up a specification of performance, which must be based on a reasoned assessment of what performance level will satisfy the requirement of fitness for purpose. Once a specification is established, quality can be said to be a matter of ensuring conformance to specification.

There are other ways of thinking about quality. Reliability is a criterion which has already been mentioned in relation to motor cars. In some products – auto-pilots for aircraft, for example – reliability is absolutely vital. Customer satisfaction is another type of test for quality which can be measured fairly objectively in things like food products. In theory, if the product conforms to specification it should be sufficiently reliable for its purpose and should satisfy the customer, but combined together, these other criteria provide a check on the suitability of the specification.

A similar way of defining quality, relevant to some types of industry, is in terms of conformance to the *customer's* specification. But there are two serious weaknesses in this and in any other definition which is based on conformance to a specification:

- It sets a level which is considered to be 'good enough'.
- It results in an emphasis on inspection. All the work goes into ensuring that nothing goes out of the door which does not meet the requirements of the specification.

All too often this approach to quality simply results in an army of inspectors and mountains of scrap.

A more comprehensive definition of quality is given by another of the authors on classical quality control, A. V. Feigenbaum, in his book 'Total Quality Control'. Here, quality is described as "an effective system for integrating quality improvement efforts of the various groups of the organisation, so as to provide products and services at levels which allow customer satisfaction." This definition contains several key ideas:

- Integration – pulling together the different interests in quality.
- Improvement – a dynamic view of quality which contrasts with the static idea of conformance to a specification.
- Different groups – the organisation is seen not as totally homogeneous, but as having its own internal 'suppliers' and 'customers'.
- Services – not products only, but all the services supporting them. The product itself may be entirely a service, as in an airline.
- Customer satisfaction – the consequence of the preceding steps.

The most important new feature in this definition is that

it goes beyond the idea of quality as simply a question of meeting a fixed specification, a notion which has the disastrous psychological effect of setting a top limit beyond which quality does not need to be improved. Feigenbaum's definition also removes the emphasis away from inspection and the filtering out of defective products.

THE OBJECTIVE OF TOTAL QUALITY

The central objective of Total Quality is to eliminate waste by cutting manufacturing variance to the minimum

In this book we should like to go still further, and, while accepting all the above as elements in our total understanding of quality, we would cite as the central objective of a Total Quality policy *the elimination of waste by the minimisation of manufacturing variance*. Reducing manufacturing variance, which expresses quality improvement in a measurable form, may require some additional spending, but its effect is the elimination of waste.

Take a simple example. In the food processing industry there is a requirement to fill cartons or bottles to a certain minimum weight. Allowance has to be made for some variation in the 'turn of scale', but anything over the minimum weight puts extra cost into a product the price of which is already fixed. With some food products any extra weight can thus result in substantial additional costs, anything which can be done to reduce the variation from one carton to the next will therefore have an immediate result in cost savings.

A similar situation occurs in raw material processing, where plate or tubing is delivered by weight or by length. If you are delivering by weight, you may want to roll or draw material close to the top end of the thickness tolerance scale in order to minimise the work needed to get it to size. If on the other hand you are delivering by length, you may prefer to operate at the lower end of the thickness scale to save material. Reduction of manufacturing variance thus opens up new opportunities for reducing costs.

In machining-type operations, if you can cut down on

variations between parts, you will be able to reduce the amount of inspection. Indeed, beyond a certain point you may be able to eliminate inspection altogether, with the prospect of considerable savings. If you have a process which is 99% within specification, you may well have to inspect the output, because conformance to specification is critically important. However, if you can get this level up to 99.95%, it may be possible to reduce the rate of inspection drastically. In that case, although the effect on the amount of scrap and rework is small, the overall cost saving can be immense.

JUST-IN-TIME

Total Quality and JIT both start with the aim of eliminating waste

The central feature of our approach to Total Quality is therefore the elimination of waste in order to increase competitiveness. It is almost exactly the same approach as would be taken in launching a Just-in-time (JIT) project. Both types of investigation start from this same point of waste elimination and have a great deal in common.

Whether you consider Total Quality or JIT first as a solution depends on where your main problems and opportunities are. If you see the chance to make a dramatic reduction in lead time, your first step will probably be to adopt a JIT programme and to follow it up with Total Quality. However, if your main opportunity for manufacturing improvement is through cutting the total cost of quality to your business, or if it is important to give your customers an improved perception of the quality of your business and products, then you will go for Total Quality. As you implement Total Quality more fully, though, you will find that you no longer need such large inventories, and opportunities will open up for implementing a JIT philosophy. It is no accident that the Japanese started from the Total Quality ideas of Feigenbaum and Deming and went on to develop the concept of JIT.

MANUFACTURING VARIANCE

Waste is to be eliminated throughout the business – starting with marketing

While the way to eliminate waste is through minimising manufacturing variance, this does not mean focusing only on what happens in the production shops. Variance can be generated throughout the entire manufacturing business. Fig. 2.1 is a simple representation of the whole manufacturing cycle, showing the different functions which have an influence on quality.

To begin with, let us consider *marketing*. If you sell the customer the wrong product for his or her purposes, you have failed from the beginning, and manufacturing it for him or her will be an expensive mistake.

For example, with the benefit of hindsight, the BAC Trident aircraft was probably one of the industry's biggest mistakes. It was originally intended to be a much larger aircraft, for which Rolls-Royce was to develop the Medway engine. However, the major customer, BEA, decided the aircraft was too big. The Medway was scrapped and Trident was scaled down and equipped with three Spey engines. The troubles then began. First, no other customers wanted it because it was too small. Then BEA itself decided that it was too small, but ended by having to use a government subsidy to buy the modified Trident, to avoid having to buy Boeing 727s – which were designed to almost the same specification as the original Trident.

Thus, what a customer specifies is not necessarily what he or she actually needs. But it is the supplier who suffers if he or she fails to clarify with the customer what the real need is.

This point can be underlined with another example. A British company recently sold £500,000 worth of capital equipment to a company in the USA. The selling company was sure it was the wrong machine for the job, and had told the customer as much, but agreed to supply what the customer had specified. Finally, however, the manufacturer replaced the machine free of charge, because it simply would not fulfil its function. This was a mistake in marketing. The machine was well-designed, well-built, inspected and tested. It had been shipped and installed as

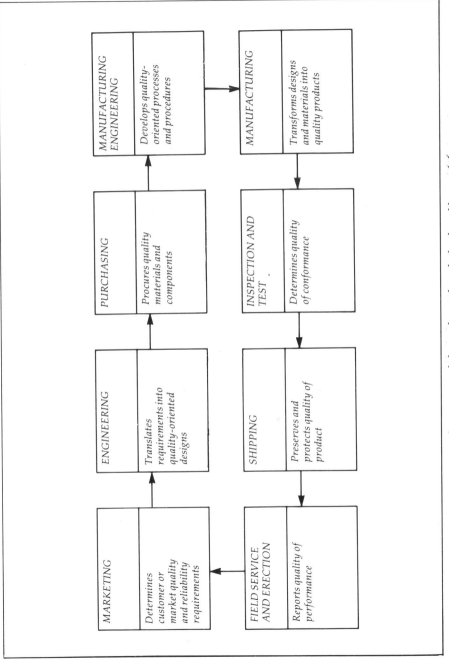

Fig. 2.1. Manufacturing variance can be generated throughout the whole closed loop of the company

carefully as possible, in accordance with the specification. But the specification itself was wrong. No amount of attention to quality at later stages can compensate for a misjudgement in marketing.

Engineering is the next stage in the manufacturing cycle. The task here is to translate the specification given by Marketing into a technical specification which the rest of the organisation can work with. Again, if this is not done correctly, and the technical specification does not accurately interpret the customer's requirements, then conformance to specification by the other departments will simply mean that the end product is wrong.

Purchasing to the lowest price can cause problems down the line

Purchasing takes the specification from Engineering and orders goods from suppliers on the basis of the specification. If it buys to the lowest price, regardless of what the specification actually says, then problems will be created further down the line. A small saving by Purchasing can lead to much higher costs for Manufacturing Engineering, Manufacturing, or Inspection and Test.

Equally, of course, Engineering can impose unnecessary costs on Purchasing by calling for special equipment where, by better design, off-the-shelf equipment could have been used. This is a quality matter, and is part of what we mean when we talk about *Total* Quality.

Purchasing is committed to obtaining the best value for money for the company, and if it finds one supplier is offering goods at half the price charged by another supplier, it needs to find out why this is the case before placing an order for the lower-priced goods.

Manufacturing Engineering provides the vital link between the engineering specification and the manufacturing departments, which may have to produce components for assembly and will have to assemble the final product. The first concern of Manufacturing Engineering must be to ensure that things are made correctly the first time. If it does not do its work properly, then the factory will be struggling.

A certain company had difficulties in boring some very

large units on its machining centres. The problem became so institutionalised that the process planning even made allowance for rectification after inspection as a standard operation. There was no mystery about the cause of the trouble: it was simply that the machining centres were incapable of holding the diameter tolerance. The logical solution would have been to take the output from the machining centres and hone all the bores. While this would have added an operation, it would also have eliminated most of the inspection, because of the inherent accuracy of honing. A better finish would have been obtained on the bore, providing a useful benefit, and the regular rectification operation would have been cut out.

It is often worthwhile to use a slightly more expensive process to ensure that quality is right first time. The uncertainty is removed and a lot of inspection and rework is eliminated.

Manufacturing – it is probably clear by now that by the time Marketing, Engineering, Purchasing and Manufacturing Engineering have been scrutinised, and steps taken to ensure that their tasks are being carried out with due attention to quality, then the actual manufacture should be a fairly straightforward task.

It is also apparent that all that has been said so far is equally relevant to a company that does not manufacture. In fact, a distribution company with no engineering or manufacturing functions can benefit equally well from a Total Quality approach.

Inspection and Test forms an almost insignificant part within Total Quality

Inspection and Test forms quite a small part of the complete manufacturing cycle and should be an almost insignificant element within Total Quality. Obviously, it can only identify fitness for purpose or conformance to specification if Engineering has given it a specification against which to check in the first place. If it starts to impose its own standards, the results can be disastrous, as for example when castings have been accepted with stress-relieving radii removed from corners. The only thing that Inspection and Test can check with any certainty is whether Manufacturing has made a mistake: it is not in a position to say if there has been an error in Marketing or Engineering.

The responsibilities of *Shipping* for timely delivery of the right goods to the correct destination are straightforward, but there are still too many goods damaged in transit.

Field service and Erection are the areas which can give a good hint of an error having occurred elsewhere in the organisation. If the chief designer is out on site dealing with problems, then something has gone awry in the earlier stages of the project. The time when he or she should be out in the field is at the beginning of the job, to find out what the customer's requirements are.

Finally, closing the loop, the experience of Field Service and Erection needs to be fed back through Marketing to the rest of the organisation. The Japanese machine-tool builder, Yamazaki, makes a practice of giving its graduate engineers five years or so in the field, and then bringing them in as section leaders in Engineering. The result is a team of people who have a much better understanding of customer requirements than their opposite numbers in many British and American companies.

ACTION SUMMARY

- What is my company's working definition of quality?
- What constitutes fitness for purpose in our product or service?
- Do we have specifications that ensure fitness for purpose?
- Do we work to defined specifications, or to informal specifications?
- Do all functions recognise their quality contributions?
- What actions do we take to ensure continual quality improvement?

You will need an answer to these questions before you can implement Total Quality.

3 THE PROBLEM OF VARIANCE

In the last chapter the aim of Total Quality was defined as the elimination of waste by minimising manufacturing variance. It was shown that the source of variance may be found anywhere in the organisation, though it may not be discovered until manufacturing is under way. In this chapter the customer's perception of quality is discussed and the meaning of 'manufacturing variance' is examined.

WHO IS THE CUSTOMER?

This is not as simple a question as it might at first seem. For the maker of Krispy Krunch cereal, the end customer is the

There may be several different groups – outside and inside the company – who must be treated as customers

child who fills his or her plate with it at breakfast. But this child is not the only person whose opinions will count. It is the mother or father who will actually buy the packet of cereal. Her or his decision will depend only partly on what the child likes. She or he will also be thinking about price, nutritional value and other factors.

But the very fact that the cereal is on the supermarket shelf, and prominently displayed, depends on a decision by the supermarket chain to stock it, and here a whole new set of considerations arises. How long is the cereal's shelf life? What return does it bring in relation to the space it occupies? How reliable and regular is delivery? How good is the advertising promotion in support of the product? Even this does not complete the picture, because a distribution company, with its own requirements as a customer, will also be involved in the supply chain between the manufacturer and the ultimate consumer.

We have taken a food manufacturer as our example, but a capital goods manufacturer or a regional health authority will have similar problems. Each will have to take into account the widely differing needs of the various groups who can be counted as 'customers'.

Even this does not exhaust the scope of what is meant by a 'customer'. As Fig. 3.1 shows, there is an important network of customer-supplier relationships within the company itself. The sales department has customers it must satisfy in Engineering, Manufacturing and elsewhere. Manufacturing Engineering 'buys' its technical specifications from Engineering, and probably has strong and highly relevant views about what is being delivered.

THE CUSTOMER'S PERCEPTION OF QUALITY

The customer's quality priorities may be very different from the manufacturer's

It is important to the success of the enterprise to understand what the outside customer considers to be good quality, and to find some means of measuring it, because what is seen as important by the customer may be very different from the priority concerns of the supplier.

Jaguar Cars makes a regular practice of telephoning 150

Internal customers	Requirements
Engineering	Order number Item specifications Modifications Special quality requirements Special packing instructions Due dates
Planning	Order number Item specifications Modifications Quantities Due dates
Production `	Order number Part number Quantity Due dates (Note: other information from Engineering and Planning)
Accounts	Order number Quantity Selling price Invoice point
Despatch	Order number Part number Quantity Delivery point

Note: This list, while based on an actual case, is not intended to be comprehensive. The contents will vary substantially between organisations.

Fig. 3.1.   Every department (e.g. Sales) has its customers with their different requirements

recent customers every month to find out what they feel about the product. The main purpose is to discover whether an error has occured anywhere in the chain from engineering of the product to its delivery and service. It also has the incidental but non-negligible benefit of giving a very good impression of the company to its end users.

British Rail recently conducted a survey among Inter-City travellers to find out what they considered to be the most important things in the service provided. If members of the company had compiled their own list of priorities, they might have put comfort and punctual arrival at the top of the list. In fact they found that these items came quite a long way down the customers' list, and the aspect that travellers were most dissatisfied with was the quality of the catering service provided.

If Inter-City services were chronically bad at timekeeping or were frequently uncomfortable these factors would no doubt have topped the list. However, because they were under control, they were taken for granted by travellers and other matters assumed highest priority.

A company delivering bulk materials by truck had a customer whose offices were adjacent to the delivery point for the material. The noise of the operation was so great that the offices were unusable during the hour it took to unload the material. The customer made frequent representations to the supplier that he should deliver outside office hours. This had an effect for a short time, but before long there would be a return to deliveries during office hours. The only reason the customer continued to deal with the company was that the supplier was in a near-monopoly situation; from the customer's point of view, the quality of the service was very poor.

SPECIFICATION AS THE BASIS OF QUALITY

Make sure that your specification matches the customer's specification

The starting-point for a technical specification is the customer's specification, whether it is supplied by the customer or prepared by the marketing department on the basis of a market study. The product may be anything from a jet engine to produce a specified thrust for a given fuel consumption at a stated level of efficiency, or a washing-machine to sell at a predetermined price with a specified performance. In either case it is the task of the engineering department to transform this customer specification, first into a technical specification defining the performance in detail, and then into an engineering specification against which the product will be manufactured.

At this stage an important quality task is verification of the design, i.e. ensuring that the technical specification matches the customer's specification, and that the engineering specification conforms to the technical specification.

For some engineering products, such as pumps and compressors, a great deal of the design effort can be reduced to standard calculations and then performed with computer assistance. Where a design is breaking new ground, it may be necessary to carry out laboratory tests or to build one or more prototypes. The engineering specification is the basis for everything that follows, and the company must therefore have the assurance that what is built to this specification will perform in accordance with the customer's specification. If there is an error at this stage, there can be no hope of rectifying it further down the line.

We have said that the customer's specification is a starting-point. It is no more than that. To achieve Total Quality the specification should be regarded not as the ultimate quality objective, but as a baseline for continuous quality improvements.

DEALING WITH VARIATIONS

Analyse every cause of variation from specification

When it comes to building a product in conformance to a specification, it is not always possible to get it exactly right, especially where engineering specifications are concerned. Indeed, even the specifications themselves assume that exact conformance may not be achieved. You may have a requirement to make a component 30mm long, but the specification will include a tolerance of perhaps $\pm 20\,\mu$m. The engineer has taken it for granted that manufacturing will not achieve exactly 30mm every time, and has allowed some latitude.

This is so patently a fact of experience that we often fail to ask the simple question: why? Why do we not always get it right first time? It is not enough to talk vaguely about 'human error' or unreliability of machines. Unless we believe some evil fate is at work, there must be reasons for failing to meet a specification, and it should be possible to discover what they are. Finding the reason for a failure is then the first step towards eliminating this cause and hence the failure itself.

This approach to dealing with errors is fundamental to Total Quality. All variations from the exact requirement are suspect, even if they are within the allowed 'tolerance'. The decision about what action to take is related to the relative costs of removing or not removing the causes of variation.

DISTINGUISHING BETWEEN VARIATIONS

The fundamental distinction – assignable causes and random variations

The first step in analysing the causes of variations is to divide them into two classes (Fig. 3.2): assignable causes and random variations.

Assignable causes are simply those where somebody has made a mistake. If someone sets the automatic weighing-machine on a packing line to operate at 458g instead of 450g, there is an assignable cause behind this error.

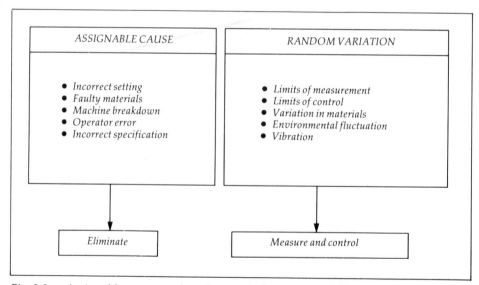

ASSIGNABLE CAUSE	RANDOM VARIATION
• Incorrect setting • Faulty materials • Machine breakdown • Operator error • Incorrect specification	• Limits of measurement • Limits of control • Variation in materials • Environmental fluctuation • Vibration
Eliminate	Measure and control

Fig. 3.2. Assignable causes and random variations require different treatment

Perhaps there was a misreading of the scale by someone who failed to appreciate fully the importance of getting it right. Perhaps there was a typing error in the specification. Perhaps – and this has been known to happen – an LED in the digital readout of the scale was defective and the crossbar of the number 8 failed to light. Whatever the reason, it can be clearly identified and put right, and steps can be taken to ensure that it does not happen again.

Random variation is more complex. There are two main types of random variation. One comprises the natural elasticities, resonances, hysteresis and so on in manufacturing equipment, which may produce some variation between one item and the next. The other consists of the many small causes of variation which may or may not be present at any time, and which taken together produce random results.

Consider for example a cylindrical grinding operation in which pieces of bar stock are ground to a certain diameter. There are many possible causes of variation, which may include temperature variations, the flexibility of the machine itself, variability in the grinding-wheel material, variations in the material being ground, errors in the automatic sizing equipment, and so on. Taken together these produce random variations in the diameter of the material being ground.

If the variations are unacceptably high, steps can be taken to deal with the individual causes. The important thing that distinguishes assignable causes from these variations is that assignable causes do not produce a random response. They result in identifiable departures from the general level of accuracy of the process, as would happen if a setting on the grinding-machine were inadvertently altered. As Sherlock Holmes might have said, when all the assignable causes have been removed, what remains is random variation.

STATISTICAL CONTROL OF RANDOM VARIATIONS

Having eradicated assignable causes, we still have not reached the irreducible minimum of variations. A new set of weapons must be deployed to reduce the variations still further. These will be examined in greater detail in Chapters 11 and 12, but a few words can be said at this stage.

We have discussed random variations. A random variation simply means there is no single obvious reason why something varies from its exact specified value. However, random variations are not completely unpredictable. It can be forecast with a high degree of confidence that the variations will not exceed a certain level.

For example, the cylindrical grinding-machine may be required to produce parts to a diameter of 20mm, and when it is working normally it may be making parts which vary between 19.97 and 20.03mm. If occasionally a piece was found to measure 20.03mm we would not be surprised, but if suddenly the machine produced a part of 20.4mm diameter we would need to look for an assignable cause.

Random variations can be monitored further by considering the frequency of each degree of variation. For example, within a band of 0.06mm around the 20mm target, we would not expect the sizes of finished parts to be evenly distributed. Most would be expected to occur within a band of ±0.01mm, practically all within ±0.02mm, and all but a very few within ±0.03mm. This commonsense view is backed up by statistical theory, which finds that if the separate causes of variations are all very small, and if they are just as likely to cause an oversize as an undersize in diameter, then out of a large number of pieces turned out by the grinding-machine, about 68% will be within ±0.01mm, 95% within ±0.02mm and 99.7% within ±0.03mm.

The word 'variance' has been used several times already in this book. This is not simply synonymous with 'variation', but is a technical expression used by statisticians to define the extent of random variations from the mean value. The term 'standard deviation' will also be used later in this book. This is the square root of the variance, and in the case we have just described, would be 0.01mm.

The key to Japan's dominance is statistical control of variation

If this reads like the sort of detailed technicality which can safely be left to somebody else, then be warned. The statistical control of variation is at the heart of Japan's present world dominance in quality manufacture. It is the message which was taken to Japan in the 1950s by the American quality control expert, Dr W. Edwards Deming. It was not a new idea even then – it had been understood and applied by a few people in the UK and the USA as far back as the 1930s. But only the Japanese took it seriously on a large scale.

It is impossible to emphasise too strongly that statistical methods are an essential element in Total Quality. The human and structural aspects which will be discussed in the next two sections of this book are important, but unless you get to grips with the statistics, you will lack the essential tools for achieving continuous improvements in quality.

Whatever the process, if all the assignable causes of variation can be identified and removed, the remaining random variations can be measured and controlled. Any event which goes outside the limits of random variation can be immediately noticed, and its cause established and dealt with.

When you have brought the process under control – that is, when you have brought it within the expected range of random variation – you can then start reducing the range of variation. You can make changes to the process and see what happens to the random variation – all with the aim of minimising the amount of variation: for example, by trying to improve the temperature control in the factory, or by setting a tighter specification for the bar stock that is bought, and so on. By measuring the variation, and the way it changes under different conditions, its causes can be isolated, and steps taken to neutralise them. This is something that cannot be achieved by merely looking at the rejects which fall outside the drawing tolerance limits.

The target – no more inspection

The prize to be gained at the end of all this effort is well worth having. By continually reducing the amount of variation, you will eventually reach the point where there will no longer be any need to carry out inspection.

The method we have described is not confined to engineering processes or measurement of variables such as weights of packages. It can be applied to any type of business task. For example, a problem involving invoicing errors can be tackled by classifying the errors into assignable causes and random variations. While there may be outright mistakes, where someone has entered the wrong information, there may also be many small errors where, perhaps, someone's handwriting is not clear, or a discount for large quantities is being interpreted differently. This type of investigation calls for a technique called attribute control, which is slightly different from the variables control used with engineering measurements. However, the general principle is the same.

QUALITY AS A NETWORK OF RELATIONSHIPS

Within a business is a network of suppliers and customers, each with different demands

The detailed analysis of individual causes of variation has been examined because this is one of the basic tools of Total Quality. It is equally important, though, to see quality in global terms as a network of relationships within and without the business organisation.

These relationships can be considered in two ways. Firstly, there are the business supplier/customer relationships mentioned earlier in this chapter, in which every department in the company has its 'suppliers' and 'customers' within as well as outside the company. Secondly, there are manufacturing process relationships, with their own sets of demands.

Consider first the *business relationships*. Each department needs to be sure, first, who its customers are, then what the customers' requirements are and how these can be measured – which may not be easy. Only then is the department able to assess whether it is performing satisfactorily and what corrective action may be needed.

In one company making one-off electronic devices, where we were advising on quality improvement, we were told that there were problems with documentation. When we looked into it, we traced the problems all the way back to sales order entry where, frankly, there was no system at all. Relationships with Engineering, Planning and other departments were informal and based on personal contacts. Documentation was haphazard and there were copious opportunities for confusion over specifications.

We had to identify at each stage what Planning required from Sales Order Entry, what Engineering required from Sales Order Entry, and so on, and we set up a straightforward system. As soon as an inquiry came in, all the paperwork was put together in a file with a 'round robin' note attached to it, and the file was circulated to the heads of Engineering, Planning, the production department involved, and the quality assurance manager. Each had to look at the job and indicate that it was satisfactory as far he or she was concerned.

When the order came in, there was a clear listing of what had to be in the file when it went from Sales Order Entry to Planning, from Planning to Engineering and from Engineering to Production. Thus, everybody at each stage knew exactly who their customer was. Sales knew that in the first instance information had to go to Planning. Planning knew it went from them to Engineering. Sales knew that certain duplicate information was passed directly to Engineering, and so on. At each stage, people knew what had to be in the file when they got it. They knew that they had a perfect right to send the file back if something was missing. There was an exception note procedure for use if information was not available.

One of the biggest problems involved outside customers who would not finalise the specification. In many cases the company could work to standards, so we instituted a procedure by which the company would telex the customer and indicate the specification to which it intended to work unless the customer called for something different. A copy of the telex was kept in the file. In this way, everyone concerned with a contract knew the information flows, who their customers and suppliers were and what information was needed from suppliers.

The company also has a network of interdependent manufacturing processes

In the *network of manufacturing processes*, there may be a first operation of cutting-off, forging or casting, followed by secondary operations such as machining, and leading into assembly. Each of these operations is defined and limited by a number of independent variables, such as the material composition of a casting, or the fundamental accuracy of a machine tool or a fixture. The outcome of each operation is a set of dependent variables, such as dimensional accuracy or surface texture, which cannot be controlled directly, but only by modifying the independent variables responsible for the outcome of the process (see Fig. 3.3).

The dependent variables from the first process then become the independent variables of the second process. For example, a casting with too little material on a surface will present difficulties in a subsequent operation if that

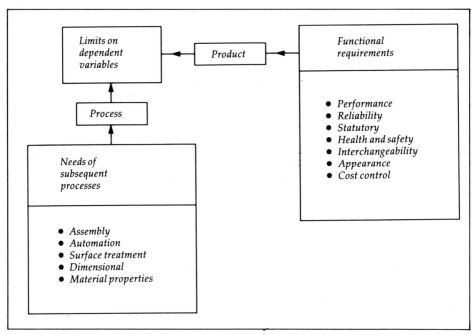

Fig. 3.3. Constraints on the requirements of dependent variables

surface has to be milled flat, and that in turn may create problems in assembly.

In order to control the independent variables of the second process – e.g. a surface which is difficult to machine correctly – the accuracy of the first process must be improved. If the traditional approach, of simply inspecting the output from the second process is adopted, a large pile of scrap is created from the castings that could not be machined satisfactorily. The customer who has to carry out the third process will have been satisfied, but by the wasteful method of filtering the output from the second process through an inspection operation.

Don't inspect – correct the upstream process

Instead, what should be done is to get to work on the independent variable – for example, dimensional variations in the casting – isolate its assignable causes and deal with them, and then monitor the process to discover whether the random variations maintain the output within limits acceptable as independent variables to the customer carrying out the second process. If they do not, further work will have to be done in the statistical control of variation.

This is a formal way of stating something that is already in operation between many manufacturing departments. All too often, though, the logic of it is not followed through rigorously and we are left with much unnecessary inspection.

Some processes cannot at present be controlled to a level which will guarantee zero defects: silicon wafer manufacture for very large-scale integrated (VLSI) circuits is an example, as are most types of casting and forging. But there are many processes which could be controlled much more closely than is commonly the case today.

If inspection is unavoidable, do it as close as possible to the source of the problem

The Total Quality task is to look at the network of manufacturing processes and distinguish between those where inspection can be eliminated and those where it will continue to be necessary, even if only as a short-term expedient. Where inspection is necessary, it should be carried out as close as possible to the source of the problem, so that the least possible value is being added to the product before a defect is discovered. For other manufacturing processes, the task is to maintain continuous control to ensure that any assignable causes are immediately identified and acted upon, and that random variations remain inside the limits of the process specification.

ACTION SUMMARY

- Who are *all* the customers for your product or service?
- Do you know what your customers mean by 'quality'?
- Do your specifications reflect the customer's idea of quality – for example customer demand for reliability?
- What are the inherent random variations of your processes?
- What are the major assignable causes of variation in your operations?
- Do you understand and use statistical methods?
- Sketch out the customer/supplier relationships in your business.
- Sketch out the manufacturing processes. Identify the location of inspection. Is this based on logic or tradition?

Answer all the above questions, or take steps to find the answers.

PEOPLE

It should be clear by now that Total Quality is not about the responsibilities of one department labelled 'Inspection' or 'Quality Control' or 'Quality Assurance'. It concerns the whole company, and requires a new approach to the company's operations at all levels of the organisation. Any development as radical as this has three dimensions – it will involve changes in people, structure and technology. The next three sections of this book will deal with each of these three aspects in turn.

It is not enough to address only one aspect, because a change in one inevitably has consequences for the others. For example, if the management of an airline decides to change it from a charter operation to a scheduled service, the nature of the task is changed, and the management will have to consider whether it has the right kind of aircraft, whether the staff who are experienced at herding large numbers of tourists will be able to adapt to cosseting first-class passengers, and whether the management structure is right for the new type of operation.

So it is not enough to run a programme aimed at changing employee attitudes without at the same time rectifying any defects in the technology and structure of the company as regards quality. It is not enough to introduce sophisticated control and measurement tools in isolation from the needs and interests of the people who will have to use them, and the organisation which will take advantage of their capability. Nor is it enough to build a quality management organisation without the necessary technological support or without harnessing the good will of the people who will be affected by it.

All three aspects are equally important, but we are starting in this section of the book with people, because it is here that top management input is most important and far-reaching in its consequences.

4 THE MOTIVATION FOR QUALITY

The chief executive must be resolved on Total Quality or the venture will not succeed

If the Total Quality approach is to be taken seriously throughout the organisation, it must be seen to be taken seriously at the top. This is the first principle which we assert in this chapter, and apply to organisation for quality in the next. You will not persuade the man on the shop-floor, or the junior draughtsman, to take full responsibility for his contribution unless he sees people higher up in the organisation acting on the same basis; and they in turn will take their cue from the top.

James Halpin, director of quality at the US aerospace company, Martin's, Orlando Division, tells in his book 'Zero Defects' about the highly successful quality improvement programme which in two years saved the company $1,650,000 in manufactured hardware costs alone. At the beginning of his description of the organisation which achieved this and many other impressive results he emphasises: "Before anything moves at all, the senior executive and top management must be convinced of the value of the programme. Without their wholehearted support, the programme cannot even begin to move." The same is true of a wider Total Quality implementation. It is only when a key person at the top of an organisation becomes convinced of the importance of Total Quality that real change can take place.

The same principle must be followed through at all levels of the organisation. A programme which is simply aimed at the immediately obvious problems of defective work produced on the shop-floor, and aims to encourage more attention to quality at that level, will at best have limited and short-term results. The biggest responsibility for quality lies with management, and it is there that commitment to Total Quality must be won before any programme can be started at supervisory or shop-floor level.

Everybody in the company must be motivated towards quality improvement

Motivating people to work for Total Quality is an important ingredient in the programme. If you believe that people are motivated only by fear or greed, then you might as well skip now to the technical section of this book. However, you will be passing up the opportunity of channelling the most powerful resources in your company in the direction of greater efficiency.

The idea of quality is a key element in what gives people satisfaction in their work. The best-known analysis of factors producing job satisfaction was that reported by Herzberg and his colleagues in 1959, after interviewing 200 engineers and accountants in Pittsburgh. They noted the factors which were mentioned by interviewees in connection with events at work about which they felt particularly satisfied or dissatisfied.

FACTORS PRODUCING JOB SATISFACTION

Five factors were mentioned far more in the context of satisfaction than of dissatisfaction:

- Achievement.
- Recognition.
- The work itself.
- Responsibility.
- Advancement.

The remaining factors – company policy and administration, supervision, salary, interpersonal relations and working conditions – were mentioned far more often in the context of dissatisfaction. The latter therefore came to be described as 'hygiene factors' – things which, if they were not right, could cause a great deal of dissatisfaction, but which at best could give only short-term positive satisfaction. A comparison of the factors associated with satisfaction and with dissatisfaction is shown in Fig. 4.1.

The positive factors, called the 'motivators', differed substantially in the duration of satisfaction which they afforded. Longest-lasting was responsibility, followed by the work itself and advancement, while achievement and recognition – which were mentioned most often – gave relatively short-term rewards. The Total Quality concept described in this book relies on all five motivators, but lays particular stress on giving people real responsibility for their work, and on satisfaction in getting the job right first time.

In the environment of Total Quality, this question of responsibility raises particular problems, because of the overriding importance of the specification. As we have said, the specification does not set a ceiling for quality, but it does establish an irreducible minimum below which quality must not fall. All work - whether it is a design or a finished product – either does or does not conform to its specification.

From a motivational point of view it is important to give people responsibility for their own work, but the customer, whether an outside purchaser or another department, has a strong interest in seeing that the responsibility is exercised to produce work in conformance to the specification. Thus, the scope at shop-floor level for individual initiative in interpreting or even improving on the specification is

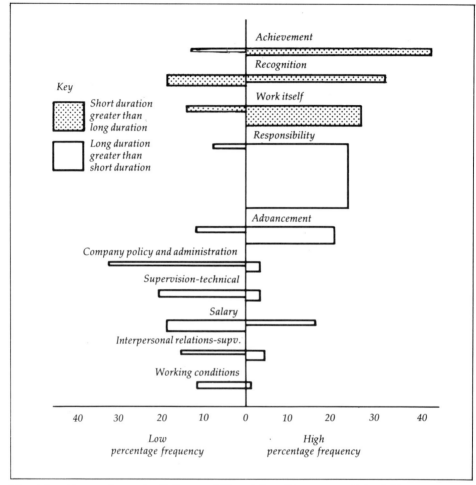

Fig. 4.1.   Comparison of satisfiers and dissatisfiers (Courtesy of John Wiley & Sons, Inc., New York)

apparently nil. All improvement proposals, particularly where they concern safety-critical products, must be accepted by Engineering.

Rigid specification is not incompatible with motivation   The very existence of a rigid specification might therefore be seen as a demotivator, limiting a person's scope for creativity and achievement. Two things can be said about this. Firstly, the fact that people cannot be allowed to make freelance departures from a specification should not be made to stifle the flow of new ideas, as long as these are first checked with the department responsible for the specification. If action to eliminate waste leads also to the opportunity for enhancing quality, for example by providing the same product performance at lower cost or better performance at the same cost, there is ample scope for achievement and recognition.

Secondly, it is easy to over-emphasise the importance of creative opportunity in work, the case for which has been most clearly put by McGregor in his discussion of what he calls 'Theory X' and 'Theory Y'. In simple terms, Theory X and Theory Y give different answers to the question 'Is man a beast?'. The assumptions behind the two theories are set out in Fig. 4.2. Theory X describes the implicit assumptions

Theory X:
- *The average human being has an inherent dislike of work and will avoid it if he can*
- *Because of this human characteristic, most people must be coerced, controlled, directed, threatened with punishment to get them to put forth adequate effort toward the achievement of organisational objectives*
- *The average human being prefers to be directed, wishes to avoid responsibility, has relatively little ambition, wants security above all*

Theory Y:
- *The expenditure of physical and mental effort in work is as natural as play or rest*
- *External control and the threat of punishment are not the only means for bringing about effort toward organisational objectives. Man will exercise self-direction and self-control in the service of objectives to which he is committed*
- *Commitment to objectives is a function of the rewards associated with their achievement*
- *The average human being learns, under proper conditions, not only to accept but to seek responsibility*
- *The capacity to exercise a relatively high degree of imagination, ingenuity, and creativity in the solution of organisational problems is widely, not narrowly, distributed in the population*
- *Under the conditions of modern industrial life, the intellectual potentialities of the average human being are only partially utilised*

Fig. 4.2.   Basic assumptions of 'Theory X' and 'Theory Y' business managers (Courtesy of McGraw-Hill Book Company, New York)

of many traditional industrial managers, against which McGregor's Theory Y offers a very different set of assumptions.

CHOOSING THE RIGHT STRUCTURE FOR QUALITY

McGregor's analysis was valuable in describing starkly what had been unthinkingly taken for granted, and in pointing out that a totally different set of assumptions would better describe people's behaviour in a different industrial environment. What it did not come to terms with was that many factors influencing human behaviour are outside the control of the industrial manager, and that some types of organisations cannot allow the full development of Theory Y management. The armed forces are an obvious example, and within the manufacturing industry also there are situations, of which conformance to specification is one, where the scope for exercising 'imagination, ingenuity and creativity' is severely restricted.

Since McGregor's influential analysis, there have been several studies of business organisations which have highlighted the diversity of structures and management styles which can be successful in different circumstances. Equally, there are many different ways in which the rigid demands of a specification can be accommodated.

The most important factor is to ensure that people are made the first consideration. Harley Davidson, the US motor cycle manufacturer, recognised when it set about turning round its business that it would need to adopt the Just-in-time method, and that as a first step it would have to introduce statistical process control. But before even that it had to secure the cooperation of its employees through quality circles, and it adopted the slogan 'People first, process next, system last'.

Sport provides vivid examples of different ideas about what gives satisfaction. In a rowing eight, the scope for each member to exercise independent judgement and creativity is almost nil. He or she cannot see where he or she is going. Unless his or her boat is in the lead, he or she cannot even see the opposition. Yet it would be foolhardy to claim that a rower was less highly motivated than, say, a rock climber who has almost total freedom in deciding how he or she is going to tackle a rock face.

Quality decisions need to be made at the level of greatest expertise

The significance of these issues in relation to quality and adherence to specification will be demonstrated in the next chapter, but it is clear that different companies will need to structure themselves according to the needs of their environment, such as the type of market in which they operate, and key decisions about quality will need to be taken at the places and levels where there is greatest expertise in dealing with them.

One more piece of experimental research is worth quoting before we move on to look at the practical consequences. This is the famous Hawthorne experiments, reported by Elton Mayo in 1933, which pioneered all the subsequent sociological and psychological research into human relations in industry and which is still relevant to the motivation of groups within the factory. Mayo's work started as a conventional work study approach to the effect of different levels of illumination on the output of a group of operatives. His observations were upset by the discovery that output increased regardless of whether lighting levels were raised or lowered, and also increased in a separate control group of operatives for whom the lighting remained constant throughout the experiment.

After prolonged experimentation, all of which produced similar results, Mayo came to the realisation that production had increased because of a change of attitude in the women who were the subject of the experiments. Because somebody was showing interest in their work, and it appeared to be important, their attitude to authority had changed.

Make sure group leaders have the same aims as the company

Particularly relevant, though, to what we shall be saying about group working for quality was a later experiment with what was described as the Bank Wiring-Room Observation Group. This was a group of 14 men – nine wiremen, three soldermen and two inspectors – who were paid on a group basis. Contrary to the experience with the

other groups, production remained steady throughout the period of observation, and it became clear that each member of the group was restricting his output despite the opportunity for the group to earn more by higher production. They formed a coherent, informal social group with its own leaders and with aims quite different from those of the company. In the earlier groups no such structure had been established, and the observers themselves had therefore unintentionally been given what was in effect a leadership role.

The existence of such informal groups has been well-documented by subsequent writers, and company managers need to be sure, in setting up quality improvement groups, that their leadership has the same objectives as those of the company.

ACTION SUMMARY

- Is senior management committed to Total Quality?
- Are your Total Quality objectives (e.g. customer satisfaction, conformance to specification, reduction of variance) clear to all your people?
- Does management action reinforce or contradict these objectives?
- Are you a 'Theory X' or 'Theory Y' organisation?

Answer the above questions, then:

- Define the type of environment of your business.
- Describe the type of organisation which meets the demands of that organisation.
- Write down what you have to do to create that environment.
- Do it!

5 RESPONSIBILITY FOR QUALITY

A quality manager we once knew was called in to the production director's office and told that the factory was producing too much scrap. The quality manager was really no more than a chief inspector, and he said "What am I supposed to do about it? I don't make it, I only inspect it." The production director's response was "Well, see about it anyway."

The production director was right, but for the wrong reason. His coded message to the quality manager was "Do you really have to be so strict?." What he should have been saying was "Your job is not to sit there and stop things from getting past you, it is to help the production people improve quality."

APPORTIONING RESPONSIBILITY

Quality is the responsibility of line management

In Japanese factories they do not even have a quality department: quality is the responsibility of line managers. There is sound reasoning behind this. If you set up a separate department or function with responsibility for quality, it has the effect of taking that responsibility away from the line management, so that the line manager becomes relatively uninterested in the quality of production. There are two reasons for this loss of interest. The obvious one is that, even if a requirement for quality is listed in the line manager's job description, he or she knows that the ultimate responsibility lies with somebody else. But there is also a psychological factor which can be found in any situation where one person's work is inspected by another: a resentment, which may be unconscious, of the other person's status.

The quality manager's role is to support, train, motivate – and monitor performance

So is there a role for a quality manager? Yes, there is, but it is not a direct or sole responsibility for quality. The quality manager has the primary task of helping the line managers to carry out their quality improvement responsibilities effectively. At the policy level, the quality manager should have some important input to the company's strategic planning and business planning. There is is also a major responsibility for training and motivating people at all levels. In addition, there is a 'scorekeeping' role – keeping people informed of their performance compared with specifications, quality costs and other measures, as well as budgeting for future preventive action against defects. There is a key role in vendor quality assurance, and most important of all, in representing the customer to the company.

If line managers are to be held responsible for quality, this duty must be taken seriously. They must be given the authority and power to take control of quality. They must be made accountable for its exercise.

SETTING QUALITY TARGETS

The status of quality among all the demands made on your managers' time and effort must also be established. If you set a budget and production targets and expect your managers to keep to them, and then add 'And by the way, please do something about quality', it will be quite clear what you really think about quality. Managers must have a clear target against which to measure their achievement. It must be a realistic, quantifiable target, they must have the power to take action towards achieving it, and their results must be measured – and taken as seriously as performance in other areas.

Quality targets must have priority and reflect the customer's requirements

In Chapter 8 the whole subject of quality costs, targets and measurement will be discussed, but it must be emphasised here that quality targets should reflect the relationship of the manager's department with its customers, whether inside or outside the company (Fig. 5.1). Quality targets should usually be expressed as costs, in order to put them on equal terms with other targets assigned to the manager. In production departments, though, it may be more realistic to use a simple physical measure of waste or scrap.

Who should set managers' quality targets? The same principles apply as in setting other types of targets, but there are some special considerations because quality is concerned with the supplier/customer relationship. Managers should be involved in setting their own targets, otherwise they will not consider themselves fully committed to them. But their customers also have an interest in their targets, and should be represented when objectives and targets are being fixed. This leads directly to the idea of group working for quality, and underlines the fact that group working is not just a matter for quality circles at shop-floor level.

As long ago as 1961, Likert pictured a company organisation as a linked network of groups (Fig. 5.2). Each group consists of a general manager with all the other managers reporting to him or her (shown enclosed by a triangle in the figure). At the top of the company is the chief executive with the top management team. At all other levels in a medium or large company, each manager is a member of two groups – the one coordinated by the next senior manager, and the one for which he or she is

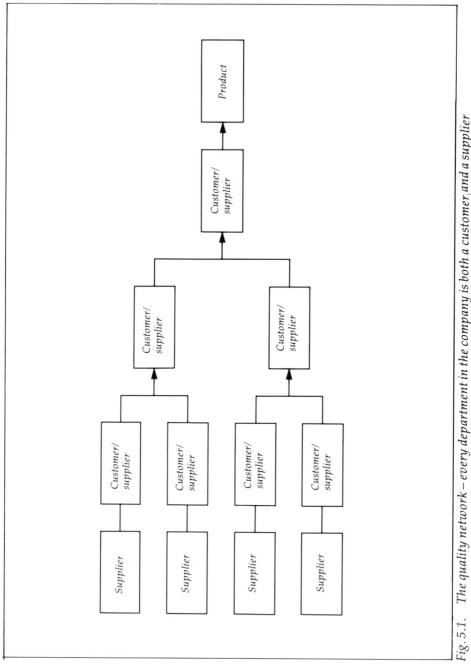

Fig. 5.1.   *The quality network – every department in the company is both a customer and a supplier*

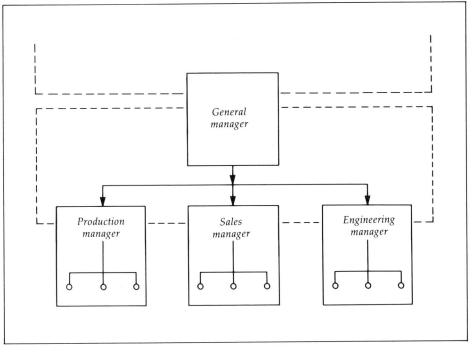

Fig. 5.2. Every organisation is a linked network of groups

individually responsible. A great deal of management teaching and writing has focused on the dynamics of these groups, and on the role of the leader in setting and maintaining group objectives, and in supporting the needs of the group and of individuals. At Rank Xerox, as we saw in Chapter 1, these groups are described as 'family groups', operating right through the company.

Quality objectives should be hammered out within these groups, starting from the top of the company. Then all the internal suppliers and customers will confront each other, and their inevitable conflicts of interests can be resolved at the appropriate levels. If the marketing director, the sales director, the engineering director and the production director can agree on their policies for quality, there is a foundation for establishing responsibilities for quality further down the line. If they cannot agree, then Total Quality is a non-starter.

PERSONAL RESPONSIBILITY FOR QUALITY

Specifications must be clear and unambiguous

Personal responsibility for quality within the area under a person's control is carried right through to supervision and to individual operators in the factory. Crucially important in the factory is the specification. Everybody must clearly understand its purpose. For example, in one company, a special casting was made for a machine and was found not to fit. This was particularly inconvenient because the machine was needed to complete an urgent order, and there was therefore a tense situation between the sales director and the production director.

The production director demanded a replacement casting with an absolute guarantee that it was correct to drawing tolerances. The part was made, and the guarantee given by the chief inspector, but the new part still did not fit. When it was measured, it was found that the 'as-cast' dimensions did not conform to the drawing tolerance. It was also obvious that the tolerance was unrealistically tight for the size of the component.

The truth then emerged that within the corporate culture of the factory there was an unwritten rule that a component was deemed to be correct to drawing if all the machined dimensions were within tolerance. The production director was not aware of this, so that when the chief inspector told him the part was correct to drawing, there was a complete failure of communication.

If such misunderstandings can occur at the level of chief inspector, the importance of giving people clear and unambiguous specifications, and not relying on their idea of fitness for purpose, is obviously critical.

A good specification embodies the experience of technologists and scientists in a form which can be applied by people with much more limited experience. The counter staff at MacDonalds hamburger restaurants do not usually have degrees in food science, but they do know that cooked meat is thrown out if it is not sold within eight minutes. They are conforming to a clear specification which has been written to safeguard the quality of the product. To know exactly how long a hamburger could be safely kept in particular circumstances would require a much higher level of qualification and knowledge.

Only if the people at the machine or the assembly bench have been given a clear and unambiguous specification can they be held responsible for their work (Fig. 5.3). Management must also ensure that they have the tools necessary for doing the job. This will be further discussed in the 'Technology' section of this book (Chapters 10 – 12).

Give people the right tools – and make them responsible for their work

This is the point at which many companies get cold feet, and say in effect "We are making you responsible for getting your work right, but we are going to inspect the work to make sure you get it right." This amounts to saying that the company does not trust its own people. This is not a good motivator, and also adds to the cost of the product. On the other hand, some kind of monitoring is needed to protect the interests of the downstream customer, who may be the person buying the company's product.

Several approaches have been tried by different organisations to resolve this dilemma. A method adopted within British Telecom is typical, and provides a good example. It is called 'delegated release', and is offered to employees who have proved to be consistent over a period of three months in identifying good and bad work in their output. This is quite different from saying they produced

---

- *Clear specification of requirements*

- *Suitable production equipment*

- *Suitable gauging*

- *Adequate training*

- *Acceptance of responsibility*

- *Auditing*

Fig. 5.3.   Essential conditions for operators to be given responsibility for their work

100% good work, since the quality of tooling or other factors may make it difficult to achieve zero defects. With such employees, the company offers an agreement which allows them to inspect their own work. It provides them with an acceptance stamp, thus giving them the status of inspectors.

The company must be absolutely honest about the quality of the tooling and equipment supplied for employees' use. If it is not good enough to produce work which is always within specification – in which case inspection would not be needed anyway – the company must explicitly acknowledge that there will be a proportion of defective work, and it is the employees' responsibility to separate out the work that does not conform to specification.

It is normal in these circumstances to carry out a random audit. This could again be interpreted as a lack of trust, but it could be better described as trust with occasional verification, and the same approach is adopted with managers in giving them targets and scoring their performance against those targets. The audit, once again, is not to find out how much bad work has been produced, but to check that the employee has clearly identified what is good and what is defective in the output.

Companies that have tried this approach have found that it works. It has been adopted even in areas where there are safety-critical products and where government quality assurance directorates are involved. Provided the operator meets the requirements for being an inspector, he or she is classed as an inspector, and the fact that he or she has also produced the work is incidental.

QUALITY IMPROVEMENT GROUPS

Total Quality is not simply about conforming to specification, but about continual improvement beyond the demands of the specification. It could be dangerous to allow people on the shop-floor to make freelance adjustments to the processes for which they are responsible, however well-intentioned they may be. How, then, can the valuable experience of the people who are closest to the manufacturing processes be enlisted, and their participation in the process of quality improvement be encouraged?

Much has been said and written during the past few years about quality circles, or quality improvement groups, and their role in raising the quality performance of Japanese industry. Many companies have experimented with quality improvement groups, but in a good proportion of cases the programmes either failed to materialise, or petered out after a relatively short time. Nevertheless, quality improvement groups were reported last year to be in operation at between 400 and 500 different work sites in the UK, and where they are successful there is a good deal of praise for them and for the advantages they bring (Fig. 5.4).

Why some quality improvement groups fail

Why do quality improvement groups succeed in some places and fail in others? A series of surveys carried out by the University of Manchester Institute of Science and Technology (UMIST), UK, were reported and analysed by

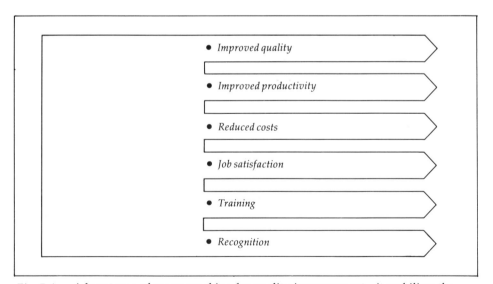

- *Improved quality*
- *Improved productivity*
- *Reduced costs*
- *Job satisfaction*
- *Training*
- *Recognition*

Fig. 5.4.   Advantages of group working for quality improvement – it mobilises the whole workforce behind the project

Ron Collard and Barrie Dale in *Personnel Management*, February 1985. Some of their findings matched the thesis of this book very closely, confirming that concern about quality must start at the top of the organisation and be accepted with conviction through the levels of middle management. Only then can the idea of responsibility for quality begin to be introduced at shop-floor level – whether it is individual responsibility, or group responsibility through quality improvement groups.

Why quality improvement groups are well worth the time and effort invested in them

Why introduce quality improvement groups? Companies interviewed in the UMIST studies talked more about employee job satisfaction than about improving quality, and more about better communications than about cost savings and greater competitiveness, though all of these were cited as reasons.

Another factor is that such groups use untapped resources. We recently visited a firm which had 50 different production lines, and management were concerned that there were improvement opportunities which they were not taking. They had set three graduate trainees to work on one of the lines, and they were getting some useful results. The graduates were not using any techniques which were outside the scope of a quality improvement group – and there were still another 49 lines awaiting attention. The only way of building resources to tackle a job of such a size is to make use of the abilities of the people on the production lines – abilities which are considerably greater than most managers are prepared to admit.

The most likely source of opposition to quality improvement groups is middle management

Quality improvement groups must be championed from the top of the company. The UMIST authors point out: "Top management should be crystal clear as to why it wants them, because, from our experience, some managers will always object to them. In 35 out of 132 manufacturing companies surveyed, management raised nine types of objections, the two main ones being scepticism about the merits of the latest in a series of vogue management techniques (40%), and worries about a loss of management control (28%)." If managers remain unconvinced or feel threatened by quality improvement groups, there are many discreet ways of proving that they are unsuccessful.

Trade union opposition has been encountered by some companies, but this has often been because the purpose of the groups has been misunderstood. Where groups are clearly presented as benefitting the company as a whole, and not as another management technique, trade union members have proved cooperative and have participated in and led quality improvement groups.

One of the surest ways to prevent a quality improvement groups programme from succeeding is to fail to provide and train a facilitator who will support and give training to the individual groups. The tasks of the facilitator are summarised in Fig. 5.5. The UMIST studies showed clearly that the success of a programme was directly proportional to the facilitator's input. Where there was no facilitator there was the highest risk of failure.

Training is a requirement which cannot be evaded or skimped on

Training is another essential condition for success. If you take a group of shop-floor workers who have never before been to a committee-type meeting, except perhaps a union meeting, and expect them to form a group and do something useful, you may be disappointed. They may have to be trained in skills such as understanding the purpose of a meeting, active participation in and running of meetings. Our experience has been that with meetings where the shop-floor people have been trained, managers are astounded at the amount of work they get through in an hour. The reason is that everyone has come to the meeting prepared, the agenda is there so that they know

- *Provide a link with senior management*

- *Coordinate improvement group activities*

- *Provide access to specialist help*

- *Ensure management respond to improvement groups*

- *Make practical arrangements for meetings*

- *Monitor success*

Fig. 5.5.   Role of the facilitator in improvement groups

what they are going to talk about, the meeting is strictly controlled, and it stops when it is supposed to. To put it bluntly, most managers have not been trained in running a meeting and so make a hash of it.

The role of the group leaders is outlined in Fig. 5.6. Further training for group leaders covers problem-solving skills, brainstorming, cause-and-effect diagrams and other techniques outlined in Chapter 6. Once again, the results can be surprising to management, and can also prove threatening unless the managers themselves have been through a problem-solving course. This is another reason for the top-down approach to group working for quality improvement. Managers should at least be given a short refresher seminar on techniques which they may or may not have learned and may or may not have forgotten, before they are brought face to face with their subordinates using such techniques.

Membership of the groups should be voluntary

It is important that membership of such groups should be voluntary. There can, though, be some flexibility in the way the 'voluntary' principle is exercised. People are not usually good at volunteering, and those who do volunteer are not necessarily the most suitable. There is no loss of the voluntary principle if the leader approaches likely members and suggests to them that they might like to volunteer. Getting the right people in the group greatly helps the cohesiveness and effectiveness of a team, but it is also important to avoid excluding anybody who wants to join.

- *Communicate about improvement groups throughout the work area*

- *Set up the group in his/her area of responsibility*

- *Chair improvement group meetings and provide leadership*

- *Develop the skills of group members and allocate tasks*

- *Make practical arrangements for meetings*

- *Liaise with project leader on provision of specialist help*

Fig. 5.6. Role of quality improvement group leaders

Where an improvement group is generating useful ideas, it should have access not only to experts within the company but also, where appropriate, to customers and suppliers. For example, a shop-floor group in the Automotive Electrical Division of Hancock Industries Group in the USA was looking for ways of improving its manufacture of cable harnesses for Ford motor cars. The factory was in Mexico, and the harnesses were being made to blueprints and delivered to Ford in Detroit. A very lively meeting with Ford representatives led to the proposal that Ford should send a car body to the Mexico factory, so that people in the shop could see and deal with the practical problems of harness wiring on the spot. The result was a marked improvement in the morale of the group and in the quality of the harnesses.

Fig. 5.7 offers a checklist of the essential conditions for the successful introduction and operation of quality improvement groups. Every one of these is important if the exercise is to prove successful. If for any reason any of these conditions cannot be satisfied, then it is probably not worthwhile proceeding with the improvement groups programme.

ACTION SUMMARY

Answer the following questions:

- Who is the person most responsible for quality?
- Should the quality manager really be called chief inspector?
- Do line managers set their objectives for quality improvements?
- Do shop-floor staff have clear specifications to work to?
- Why cannot operators be allowed to inspect their own work?
- Do you involve shop-floor staff in quality improvement?

Now:

- Ensure that the chief executive officer recognises his or her role.

1 *Secure the commitment of the board and senior management by explaining the objectives and seeking an understanding that commitment means providing resources for training, allowing meetings in working time, and making themselves available for the presentations of circles when appropriate – and all this on a long-term basis;*

2 *Involve middle management and supervision – it is essential to brief this group and to encourage willing supervisors to participate in and form circles. In addition, this group should provide specialist help to circles. Successful involvement of middle management and supervision has been found to strengthen their role and assist their relations with the shop-floor by encouraging greater contact and communication;*

3 *Seek support of trade unions – in a unionised environment it is important as a minimum to brief the trade union representative to allay suspicion and if possible to seek the union's active support;*

4 *Delegate decision making – in many organisations there will be a need to develop an understanding that for quality circles to operate successfully, decisions will need to be taken at the lowest practical level and that circles themselves, after agreement of management, will have the authority to implement changes. However, where a circle proposal needs a high-level decision, then the circle must be allowed to present its proposals to the level of management which can make the decision and do so promptly;*

5 *Provide adequate training – experience has shown that this should consist of two levels. Firstly, detailed training of potential circle leaders, usually over three days. The second level consists of providing training in a structured way to the circle in its first meetings. This would normally be done by the trainer who will also advise and counsel the circle leaders as necessary;*

6 *Use a pilot study approach – this allows evaluation and enables circles to start work without a blaze of publicity which may result in suspicion;*

7 *Monitor results on an on-going basis – the long-term development of quality circles from the pilot study stage to wider introduction will only succeed if circles reinforce their work, particularly in involving other employees in implementing change. It has often been found that if circle members talk directly to their fellow employees there is a greater likelihood of acceptance of change.*

Fig. 5.7   Conditions for successful introduction and operation of quality improvement groups (Courtesy of Ron Collard of Coopers & Lybrand and Dr Barrie Dale of UMIST)

- Develop a job description for the quality manager, emphasising education and support.
- Work with line managers to agree improvement targets.
- Remove constraints to operator control.
- Examine the opportunity for quality improvement group programmes, and introduce them where appropriate.

6 TEACHING TOTAL QUALITY

Total quality begins and ends with education

Kaoru Ishikawa, the Japanese professor who has contributed extensively to the development of quality skills in Japan, is enthusiastic about the principle that Total Quality begins and ends with education. In some areas of manufacturing, such as MRPII (manufacturing resource planning) for example, it has become a cliché that the technology is not the issue. In Total Quality, as we will go on to explain, the technology is very much the issue. However, unlike the technology of computer numerical control (CNC) or flexible manufacturing systems (FMS), it cannot be bought as a black box, but must be developed in the minds of everyone in the organisation. It is through education that the technologies of Total Quality are brought into application by people, but of equal importance is the use of education to motivate people to use the technologies.

The words education and training are often used interchangeably. In this book we make a distinction. Education is about the learning of principles, and training is about the learning of practice. In more practical terms, education is about what the organisation is doing and why, and training is about what individuals are going to do and how they will do it. It is most important to get the correct balance of education and training. It is education which motivates people to put the training into practice. The successful application of skills cements this with the motivation to continue using them. People who are used to working in a practical way often find discussion of principles unhelpful. It is desirable for sessions to end with a practical task, for example 'Go away and check that all your measuring equipment is calibrated'; or 'Make a list of all the customers for all your activities, and alongside each, list all the things they require from you'. The action summaries at the end of each of the chapters in this book fall into this category.

At this point we will keep to our own rules and give a practical example. In one company we found that there were no inspection records whatsoever. To say the least, this made any form of analysis-driven improvement very difficult. It also caused problems with the company's main customer. The difficulty was compounded by the fact that it was a very old and traditional company, where the inspectors had a firm belief that they were not clerks and that it was not their business to do any writing.

First of all we carried out an education exercise. We talked to the inspectors about Total Quality, and pointed out that by keeping records we could identify the causes of problems and prevent them from recurring, rather than inspecting out the same faults again and again. The task then was for the inspectors to help us design a system of inspection records. Once we had developed a simple recording card, we went into the training sessions. The inspectors were taught how to use the cards with the help of examples. This was followed up with further training on the shop-floor, and additional training was provided for any inspectors who were having difficulties. In the education they had learned why the improvements had to be done, and their commitment was obtained. The training ensured that they then knew how to apply their new knowledge.

There is an old saying along the lines of 'I was told and I forgot, I saw and I remembered, I did and I understood'. This is a good guide for Total Quality education and training, which is not a classroom exercise designed to get people through examinations: instead, people should seek to apply the things they have learnt, and that means that they must understand those things. The programmes therefore include as little passive listening as possible. Short 15 – 20 minute presentations are used to convey basic ideas. Participants in the programme then have to apply their knowledge practically. The details and practicalities are discovered in exercises, which should be as close to the daily realities of the business as possible. At the end of the exercise, which might last for an hour or so, the teacher will spend half-an-hour helping the participants to bring out the lessons which have been learned. At times this may seem a slow way to proceed, but it has the great advantage that the levels of understanding and retention are very high.

THE LEARNING PROCESS

Teaching will start at the top and be driven through the whole organisation

The first steps in the education and training process within a company are usually varied, and are probably highly dependent on chance. An influential member of the organisation may hear a conference speaker, read a book or see a television programme about Total Quality. Once an initial interest has been created, education and training in Total Quality starts from the top and spreads downwards through the whole organisation. If a company takes Total Quality seriously, then this will set the direction for the whole business. Direction should come from directors, so it is vital that they understand what they are letting themselves in for.

Education and training for directors and senior managers should take the form of a three-day off-site programme. The content of the three days is much the same as the content of this book. It should include the concept of what is meant by quality; how responsibility for quality is carried by everyone; what types of systems and structures are needed to ensure product and service quality; what the true cost of quality is to the business; and what tools and techniques are available to improve quality. As with all this work, there should be a practical outcome. At the end of the three days the directors should have produced an outline plan for the introduction of Total Quality within their business.

Further education and training should be structured to support the overall programme of introducing Total Quality. This will depend on the outline plan and priorities set out by the senior management. Any proposal to introduce quality management systems along the lines of BS5750 or ISO9000, or technologies such as improved metrology or statistical process control, or a system of quality circles or improvement groups, will require education and training. While the detailed content of the education and training programmes will vary, there are common factors in the way such programmes are structured. They usually comprise three levels:

- The management level, which gives managers enough understanding of the techniques to exploit them.
- The technical level, which gives a detailed understanding to those responsible for using techniques and training others.
- The shop-floor level, which gives staff enough understanding to work with the appropriate techniques.

In improvement group introduction, the work at shop-floor level is practically the same as at the technical level. By contrast, in some of the more advanced statistical techniques, a full technical course for engineers would require eight days, while management needs would be covered in one day, and shop-floor needs in perhaps two hours.

In all these education and training programmes it is important that both aspects are covered. Education explains why the project is being carried out, whether it is to introduce BS5750, improvement groups or any other system or technique. Training then covers the detailed activities required, and how people are expected to perform them.

Teaching programmes must point to practical actions

To give a fuller picture of an education and training programme, we will now give a more detailed example. The case we have chosen is the introduction of improvement groups at shop-floor level. These have already been discussed in the previous chapter. Improvement groups are a valuable means of getting education in Total Quality to the shop-floor. It has already been pointed out that practically-minded people need to put principles into practice if they are to have any effect. The use of an improvement group programme allows the general principles of Total Quality to be put across in a way that enables people on the shop-floor to participate actively in the process of continuous improvement. Without improvement groups or something very similar, it can be difficult to implement Total Quality at shop-floor level.

Once the commitment of top management has been obtained, the first stage of an education and training programme for improvement groups is to prepare course material which is relevant to the workplace of the participants: there is no point in using material that is appropriate to a Midlands metal-working company to try to teach Total Quality in a Cornish frozen food factory.

The next step is to educate and train the group leaders. These people are crucial, as it is they who will pass on the skills they learn to their groups. The programme for the group leaders normally involves three days off-site. These days are not easy. Their objective is to equip the group leaders to train and run their own groups. The work starts at eight o'clock in the morning, and we have known groups to be still working on the exercises at up to five o'clock the next morning, before starting again at eight! This indicates the enthusiasm which can be generated by such courses.

At the same time as the supervisory courses, short one-day seminars are held for senior and middle management, at which the same techniques are reviewed in less detail. These seminars have three important purposes:

● To tell managers what will happen at shop-floor level when the supervisor training sessions are completed.
● To avoid embarrassment for some managers who may not have encountered the problem-solving techniques which will be used by their staff.
● To prepare managers for what can sometimes be a shock, when large numbers of proposals for improvements are presented by people on the shop-floor.

The objectives of a leader training programme for quality improvement groups are summarised in Fig. 6.1. The programme for first line management and supervision goes through the basic ideas discussed in Chapter 4 regarding how people work together in groups. Participants are given practical experience within their own groups. They learn problem-solving techniques at first hand, and develop skill in obtaining a consensus within the group. They learn specific techniques like brainstorming, Pareto analysis and the Ishikawa fishbone method, and

---

- *To develop understanding of group behaviour*

- *To develop leadership abilities*

- *To improve communication skills*

- *To develop problem-solving abilities*

- *To teach leaders to train their group members*

- *To enable leaders to run effective improvement groups*

Fig. 6.1. Objectives of leader training for quality improvement groups

gain experience in using them. They also develop skills in making effective presentations and in developing suitable visual aids.

Supervisors will need support during the first few weeks of the new groups

This thorough training programme helps to give them confidence in setting up and running their own groups. It is most important to continue supporting them during the first six or seven meetings, when they will be putting most of their effort into creating effective groups and teaching them the techniques of problem solving. At each of these early sessions it is important to have a professional instructor present – not saying anything unless specifically asked, and even then contributing only minimally, but giving support to the group leader and discussing any difficulties with him or her after the meeting.

Professional instructors can be used to teach the individual quality improvement groups problem-solving skills, but this is expensive and not really desirable. It is much better to keep the instructors in the background, giving support and encouragement to the supervisors only where necessary in developing skill and confidence. In this role their presence can be extremely valuable.

Improvement groups learn by doing

At this level, as in the off-plant training sessions, learning occurs chiefly through doing. The group leader talks for perhaps ten minutes on a technique, and then sets the group a practical exercise. The leader chooses a problem which all the group members can easily understand, so that they can find out how the technique works by actually making use of it. At the same time they see that the method is powerful and relevant to their problems. The leader's task is to keep the discussion moving in the right direction, and when a solution is reached, to consolidate it and make sure the team realise how they achieved the result.

QUALITY IMPROVEMENT TECHNIQUES

Three of the most important techniques which any quality improvement group has to learn are brainstorming, Pareto analysis and the Ishikawa fishbone technique.

Brainstorming helps to generate new ideas

Brainstorming is usually the first technique to be introduced, because it gets ideas flowing and gives the group both confidence in itself and a sense of identity. If you simply ask a group of people from the shop-floor – or from middle management for that matter – to sit down and solve a particular problem, they will probably not get far. Group working does not come naturally to most people. The aim of brainstorming is to get past the usual inhibitions which stop ideas from flowing, such as unwillingness to commit oneself, fear of criticism from other people, lack of confidence in one's own judgement, and so on.

In the first stage of brainstorming, the leader offers the subject. It can be as broad as 'Let's identify our problems'. People are asked simply to share any ideas that bubble up. All comments and criticism are ruled out. Members are asked to tell their ideas, however trivial or foolish they may seem. Somebody is given a flip chart and writes down all the ideas as they come along (a lively group may need two scribes to keep pace with the ideas).

During training sessions, there are some regular subjects which have been found to be useful in stimulating ideas, such as 'List everything you can do with a paper-clip'. This can produce anything up to 100 ideas in the space of five minutes. Most of them will turn out to be trivial or ridiculous, but some will be practical and ingenious. It is a good idea for the leader to have a few slightly ludicrous ideas to throw in if the flow seems sluggish, and if there is difficulty in getting started, the leader may have to go round the room and expect everyone in turn to offer an idea. It is essential at this stage to stop any attempt at censorship or criticism of ideas as 'rubbish'. A successful brainstorming session shows an odd mixture of freedom and restraint – freedom in expressing ideas, and restraint in passing judgement on them.

The next stage is to go through the ideas which have been written down, and to classify and combine any overlapping or duplicated ideas. From this tidied list the team can decide which ideas show the greatest promise. Some surprises can happen when ideas which at first seemed unlikely are revealed as possessing the germ of a new approach, perhaps when linked with other ideas.

Middle management must be prepared for surprises at the number of problems identified

The results can be astonishing. In a typical well-run department, a quality improvement group may easily produce 50–60 problems from a brainstorming session. To a middle management team which has been telling its bosses that everything is running smoothly and is under control, this can come as a shock if the team has not been prepared for it. This is why middle management needs to be involved in the training programme and to expect such an outcome. Otherwise middle managers can quickly become hostile to the whole idea of quality improvement groups.

Pareto analysis is another simple technique of which everyone has heard, but which is not as widely understood as it should be. Pareto was a nineteenth-century Italian economist who used the method for studying the distribution of wealth in Italy. In itself it is no more than a way of presenting information. Its importance is revealed by the other name frequently given to it: 'the 80/20 rule'.

Pareto analysis separates the vital few from the trivial many

It is a common experience that the vast majority of problems can be attributed to a small minority of causes. Most of the scrap from a foundry has only one or two of many possible causes. Most of the inventory cost in a typical factory store is represented by a small proportion of part numbers. Often the proportions are 80% and 20%: 80% of scrap comes from 20% of causes, 80% of inventory cost from 20% of part numbers – but there is nothing immutable or magical about the 80 and 20. The most expensive 20% of the inventory might account for 60% or 90% of value.

This method is particularly valuable in helping the group decide where it should concentrate its efforts. When a brainstorming session generates large numbers of ideas, the rule is to go for the ones that will save the most money. It is this method of decision-making, based on attacking first the small number of most troublesome problems, which is the most important idea to get across in talking about Pareto analysis – the importance of going for the 'vital few' among the 'trivial many'.

The technique itself can be used in various ways for quality improvement. For example, a group finding out why a component or assembly keeps being rejected can list the different reasons for rejection and count the number of times each occurs. The different causes can then be arranged in order of frequency, and the cumulative totals plotted as in Fig. 6.2, to show which are the ones which should be investigated first. If the study is looking at the same range of causes for several components, it is better to use the cost of each component as a basis for comparison, because some may be much more expensive than others.

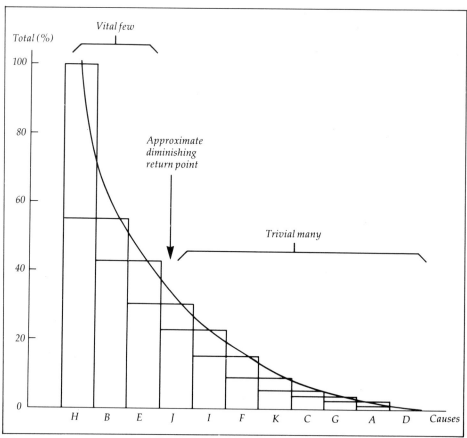

Fig. 6.2. Pareto analysis highlights the vital few troubles offering greatest potential benefits

The method can be used in many different areas. In a steel foundry, for example, it is an unfortunate fact of life that many castings need to be repaired because of porosity, tears and other causes. One technique for trying to improve the quality of a troublesome casting is to take a drawing of it and to mark on it all the places where defects have occurred. It quickly becomes apparent that 80% – 90% of the defects usually occur over about 20% of the surface area of the casting. A study of the casting itself will probably reveal the cause and so point to a possible improvement in the casting design.

Fishbone diagrams help to structure thoughts

The third simple technique which can be used to good effect by a quality improvement group is the so-called 'Fishbone diagram', introduced by Dr Kaoru Ishikawa in Japan (Fig. 6.3). This again is above all a way of structuring thoughts by representing cause-and-effect relationships in a diagram. The 'effect' – the process being studied – is represented by a line, the backbone of the 'fish'. Into this come lines representing the various factors contributing to the process. If for example the process is producing a machined component, the factors could include the material from which it is made, machine tools, cutting tools, handling operations, and so on. Each of these can then be looked at in greater detail for factors that could cause problems.

One telling example we encountered recently concerned warehousing. A warehousing business supplying supermarkets was encountering shortage of about 1% on deliveries. The amount was significant, but too small to justify expensive measures such as inspection of everything leaving the warehouse. A fishbone diagram listed such causes as people, the shift, the time of day, the area in the warehouse, the types of material, and so on. When the investigators looked further at the types of material, they uncovered the fact that coffee was the material most commonly in shortage. Coffee was a relatively high-value item, and the shortage level on it was running at about 5%.

This led to more questions. Was the shortage the same in every load? – in deliveries to every supermarket? – with all

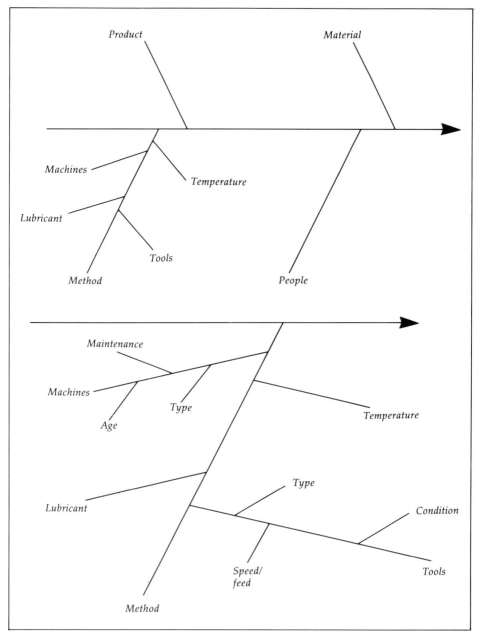

Fig. 6.3. Ishikawa fishbone diagrams for analysing cause and effect. The second diagram analyses part of the first in greater detail

the warehouse staff? Eventually, instead of trying to account for a 1% loss in a warehouse with 200 staff carrying 5,000 items, the problem was reduced to explaining a 5% loss in a known material – coffee – handled by about five people. With the problem brought down to manageable proportions, it was possible to plan further steps such as inspection, introduction of special loading procedures, or moving the handling of coffee into a special area of the warehouse.

Company managements are often surprised at the skill and confidence with which shop-floor groups use techniques such as those just described. Indeed, they handle them in a way which sometimes puts to shame the methods used by their managers.

THE SCOPE OF QUALITY IMPROVEMENT GROUPS

Various other techniques, such as paired comparisons, are also suitable for use within quality improvement groups, and some will be mentioned in the technology section of this book (Chapters 10-12), along with some techniques which demand specialist expertise. Where an improvement group is successful, it will wish to add more advanced techniques to its repertoire; if it is prevented from moving forward, it will in all probability wither and die. Statistical process control is one technique in particular which some companies have introduced very successfully by means of quality improvement groups.

The biggest quality cost-saving ideas are often beyond the scope of quality improvement groups

Before you decide that quality improvement groups are the answer to all your problems, it must be stressed that the improvements they can offer are usually limited in scope, although they are well worth having. Using the Pareto terminology, in most companies the vital 20% of quality problems causing the greatest costs come within the prerogative of management, and are thus outside the scope of an improvement group. For example, if the tools are inadequate for the job, that is something on which management must act. Alternatively, the specification may be absurdly tight. Management may not be allowing enough time, say, for curing or heat treatment. A quality improvement group may be able to identify problems like these, but correcting them is a management responsibility. The main scope for improvement groups lies in dealing with the 'trivial many' problems, which certainly should not be ignored, but are not going to bring the really big returns.

There are exceptions to this rule. Quality improvement groups can play a major role in labour-intensive, low-technology industries, where a great deal of responsibility for quality and efficiency of output falls directly on the labour force. In high-technology companies, however, the scope for such groups is severely limited, and responsibility for quality falls mainly on those responsible for the technology.

The other great value of quality improvement groups is in education, motivation and communication. The people in an improvement group become 'switched' on to the idea of quality. They know why it is necessary to meet specifications. They know the issues involved, so they are motivated to play their part in achieving the quality objectives. Although the work of the quality improvement group may be in attacking the 'trivial many' problems, its educational and motivational influence may have a considerable impact on the way the company deals with the 'vital few' problems.

ACTION SUMMARY

- Identify the awareness of quality at all levels of your business.
- Design a Total Quality briefing session.
- Carry out a senior management course (unless all your senior managers are 100% aware of Total Quality).
- Brief the company from top to bottom.
- Run one-day improvement group workshops for managers.
- Run an improvement group training programme.
- Support the operation of quality improvement groups.
- When introducing technical or structural changes, follow the same sequence.

STRUCTURE

The next three chapters are about structural aspects of Total Quality – the second of the three 'legs' on which a successful Total Quality implementation must stand. In Chapter 7 the structure of the quality management system itself is examined, and the ways in which it relates to standards such as BS5750 and its new international counterpart ISO9000 are shown. Chapter 8 concerns quality cost reporting – an important task which can be dangerous for the unwary. Chapter 9 examines in greater detail the relationships with suppliers, and concerns questions such as multiple sources, goods inward inspection and supplier quality assurance.

7 THE QUALITY MANAGEMENT SYSTEM

Quality assurance is about organising the company for continually improving quality

Quality assurance is about ensuring that the quality level is what it should be, whether in one's own company or in a supplier's products. It is concerned not simply with inspection, but also with how a company organises itself to ensure that quality is continuously maintained and improved in all its activities.

During recent years, a vast amount of experience of the procedures and systems which are necessary to give an assurance of product quality has been accumulated, and this has been codified in standards such as the British Standard BS5750, the NATO Quality Control System Requirements for Industry (AQAP), and others, all broadly similar in content and purpose.

In June 1987, the new ISO9000 series of quality standards was published, and as these come into use they can be expected to supersede the existing standards. In many respects the new standards are similar to BS5750, but there are some important differences in detail which will have to be taken into account.

QUALITY STANDARDS

In this chapter we outline the main principles involved in quality system standards. They contain much important information, condensed into a small space. The standards list many rules to be followed, and are particularly concerned with subjects such as documentation. Nevertheless, there is a close connection between such standards and Total Quality. Our aim here is not to repeat what is already set out in the quality standards, but to explain their significance to Total Quality in the light of experience in implementing between 30 and 40 quality systems in different industrial companies.

Behind the densely written text of standards such as BS 5750 lie four basic concepts:

- Eliminating assignable causes.
- Identifying and controlling random variations.
- Demonstrating the ability to produce goods to the required quality.
- Demonstrating the ability to make continued quality improvements.

A company manufacturing turbine generators for power stations imported a large rotor forging from Japan. It weighed more than 100 tons, and cost in the region of £100,000. The forging was put up on a lathe, and the operator started to machine it. He had read the drawing and assumed it was dimensioned in inch units, whereas in fact it was in metric units. Fortunately the mistake was discovered before work had gone too far, and some highly-paid design staff were set to work to re-design the whole generator so that the rotor could still be used.

This is an excellent example of an assignable cause. In

fact there were probably several assignable causes behind this near-disaster. The operator had not been adequately trained and did not have clear work instructions. He had just been transferred from working in imperial units to working in metric units and had not been taught adequately about what was involved in the change. Sufficiently clear warning was not given on the drawing, or at least he had not been taught to recognise such a warning.

Another company installed a flexible machining system for large components. When the system went into service, the engineers found that they would have to inspect all the parts being produced by it, because of the random variations in diameters of certain key features, which meant that 30% of the parts were falling outside the acceptable tolerance. The only solution to the problem was a costly one. The problem diameters were bored under size in the flexible machining system and were then taken to a manually operated machine to open them out to the correct size. The immediate cause of trouble in this instance was random variation, but there was also an assignable cause, in that the people who ordered the machining system and set it up had not adequately considered the quality issues.

A similar thing occurred in a major West German motor manufacturer with an outstanding reputation for quality. A large automation project was set up for assembling car bodies, and could not be made to work because the dimensional variations between fabrications were too great.

Eliminating assignable causes is a prime aim of BS5750

One purpose of the quality standards is to set up procedures which will help to eliminate assignable causes such as these. Long experience has shown that the vast majority of assignable errors can be traced to very few causes.

Probably the most important source of error is *documentation*. Bad documentation means that people do not know what they are supposed to be doing. They make a guess and often get it wrong. Or the documentation itself is not correct or is misleading. The specification cannot be achieved, so it is effectively ignored, and so on: hence the need for a series of requirements on the control of documentation.

Another assignable cause which turns up time and again is to do with *calibration*. People measure with equipment which has not been calibrated and which has therefore become inaccurate, or they use equipment which is incapable of achieving the required accuracy. There is therefore another series of requirements relating to the use and calibration of instruments and measuring equipment.

Inadequate *training* accounts for many assignable causes, so the standards call for management systems which anticipate problems such as confusion over metric and imperial units, as well as for thorough and well-documented training.

Quality standards lay down rules for process controls to reduce random variations

The identification and control of random variations are not so comprehensively covered by the quality system standards, but these do lay down requirements for process controls. The influential quality specification issued by the Ford Motor Company calls specifically for the use of statistical process control techniques, which will be covered in this book in the section on technology.

Detecting and acting on both random variations and assignable causes cannot make much progress unless adequate records are kept which point to possible sources of trouble. This fact lies behind the requirements in BS5750 for the keeping and analysis of records.

DEVELOPING A SYSTEM FOR QUALITY

Set a progress plan for your design work

The very first key step towards Total Quality is to achieve a design which meets market requirements. This was one factor which recurred in the case studies cited in Chapter 1, and which has been reiterated elsewhere. It should come as no surprise, therefore, that design control features strongly in the quality standards. In BS5750 there are some 11 specific requirements covering design control.

Design control is a subject which scares many people, who fear that it will cramp the designer's creativity. Properly applied design control, however, can have the opposite effect. It can release creativity by the establishment of simple procedures. The first principle proposed in BS5750 is that there should be a programme of design development. Before you start a design, draw up a programme of what is to be done, including, say, firm plans for the first three months and benchmarks for the longer term, to be revised on a regular basis.

Chapter 12 outlines the new approach to design pioneered by the Japanese engineer Genichi Taguchi, involving the three stages of system design, parameter design and tolerance design. If you use the Taguchi approach as part of your Total Quality programme, you will want to formalise it in your programme of design development.

Again, it is good practice to codify engineering standards – to specify preferred materials and dimensions, so that a draughtsman with a choice of dimensions does not simply take the first one that comes to hand. Tolerancing, calculation procedures and other such tasks should all go into a code of design practice, with procedures to ensure that everybody is working to the latest version. It should also include the administrative details of how the design function is run.

A design review ensures progress towards meeting the customers' requirements

Another key idea is that of a design review, which is quite different from a progress meeting. A design review is conducted three or four times during a design programme, to ensure that a design will be fit for its purpose and will satisfy the customer's requirements. To be effective, such a review needs to involve many people, including Marketing and perhaps the customer, besides Purchasing, Manufacturing, and so on. It will need to consider such questions as:

- Will the product do what the customer wants?
- Does it meet all the statutory requirements?
- Is it safe?
- Can we make it?
- Have we made difficulties for ourselves with any of our purchased supplies? (It has been known for a company

to rely absolutely on one supplier for a vital part, only to see the supplier go into receivership.)

Design reviews should be held at the conceptual stage of design, at detail design, at final sign-off when all the detail drawings are completed, and at the prototype stage if a prototype is built.

Unrealistic design tolerancing can destroy credibility and confidence between departments

Another important group of ideas concerns value engineering and control of tolerancing. In many companies, there are tolerances which are far tighter than anyone could possibly manufacture to. As a result, the credibility between Engineering and Manufacturing becomes totally destroyed over the years, because Engineering has imposed tighter and tighter tolerances which Manufacturing has consistently failed to achieve. What quality assurance standards call for is a system to avoid the use of irrational tolerancing.

A good way of achieving this is to take a firm grip of BS4500, which sets suitable limits and fits. There is also a useful addendum to it, BS 4500 Part 3, which gives guidance on open tolerances, where a limit or fit is not appropriate. This is worth studying closely, because some of the figures people put at the bottom of their drawings for open tolerances are the worst offenders in widening the credibility gap. A tolerance of ±0.25mm over 2m between as-cast dimensions is typical of the sort of nonsense that is written, and of course nobody tries to work to it.

Other requirements deal with new techniques and materials, the aim being to ensure that designers verify that these really are suitable and that it is not a case of seeking novelty for its own sake. Most of the design requirements are a matter of common sense. The design office that claims it cannot plan and cannot hold design reviews because it does not trust the purchasing or manufacturing departments is heading for disaster.

Quality assurance demonstrates to the customer that the supplier can meet quality requirements

The other aspect of quality systems standards concerns *quality assurance*: the guarantee which a customer requires that a supplier will deliver goods of the required quality. The implicit guarantee is given by the supplier, by demonstrating that he or she has a quality management system capable of ensuring good quality products.

The customer wants to know that you have been able to identify his or her requirements and can communicate them accurately throughout your organisation. So he or she will want to see that you have a system of controlled documentation. This is the sort of requirement that makes many senior managers feel frustrated. It appears to be demanding that large volumes of records be kept which are simply put into filing cabinets and stored in case the customer wants to check them. If this is all that happens to the documentation then it certainly is no better than an expensive exercise to satisfy the customer, and if your company is perfect and never encounters any quality problems you can afford to treat your documentation in this way. But if, like most companies, yours can still benefit from quality improvement, there is a potential profit for your company locked up in those records.

Documentation is not just for the customer's benefit – the company can profit from it too

Your customer will want to see that you have identified all the inspection and test operations that are necessary, so you will have to keep records of them. But if you yourself want to make sure that your quality system is right, this is exactly what you will need to do – and you will want to keep records and check them to ensure that your people are carrying out all the necessary inspection and test operations.

It is a sad fact that a great many factories carry out inspection and testing simply on the basis of tradition. The budget makes allowance for a certain number of inspectors, so that is the number that can be afforded and that is the amount of inspection that is done. The budgeted number was probably decided arbitrarily – the same number as last year, for example, or perhaps the same percentage of projected turnover. Almost inevitably, this means that too much or too little inspection is done: it is unlikely that a system based on such a tradition will fortuitously stumble on the correct level of inspection. The only satisfactory way of deciding what level of inspection and test is needed is to keep quality records – and these are exactly what the customer will demand in order to meet the requirements of BS5750.

Training records allow you to find out what staff training is still needed

The same applies to training records. Your customer will want to be confident that you have trained your staff in all the functions necessary to assure him or her of the quality of your output. But if you yourself want to be certain that you are producing good quality work, you will have to train your personnel. More than that, you will want to keep records of that training, so that you always know who is capable of which tasks, and who still needs further training.

It is not enough simply to lay down procedures without ensuring that they are being followed and that they are having the desired results. In Ancient Greece, Xenophon, writing about military command, said that it was normal practice that if you gave an order, you checked that it was carried out. Far too often managers give an instruction and assume that it has been implemented, when in fact there is a fair chance that it has not. Even if it has, that is not enough in a quality situation. Has it also produced the required result? If not, why not? Perhaps it was the wrong action in the first place, in which case you will have to think of something more appropriate, and you will have to go through a procedure of corrective action, checking the results, until a solution has been found which completely resolves the problem. Then you can forget about it and turn your attention to something else.

It is this approach which lies at the heart of what is meant by continued action to improve quality, and it cannot be followed through effectively without the meticulous record-keeping demanded by quality system standards such as BS5750.

THE ROLE OF THE QUALITY MANAGER

A key person in the implementation of continued action to improve quality is the quality manager. BS5750 describes this person as a 'quality management representative'. This does not mean someone who will guarantee the company's quality: it is a fundamental principle of this book that quality is everybody's responsibility.

The quality manager should not simply be the chief inspector, renamed

The quality manager's role at its simplest is to show the customers round and help them to assess the system. But the quality manager should also ideally be a centre of wisdom, a person who knows how the system works, a referee, a final arbiter. If a difficulty cannot be resolved by the quality manager, it goes to the managing director. The quality manager should be responsible for the essentials of a quality assurance system, and in particular for the documentation.

What sort of person should the quality manager be? One thing is certain: he or she should not simply be the chief inspector, promoted and called 'quality manager'. The less he or she knows about inspection and test the better, because Total Quality is not about inspection and test. What is required is a good manager who can persuade people to accept their quality responsibilities. The chief inspector is an important person, but has a different role and has been trained in different functions.

Where should the quality manager fit into the organisation? This depends on the type of organisation, but he or she should ideally be a senior manager reporting directly to the chief executive. The appointment should be at such a level that, if there are any conflicts, he or she is at the same level in the company as the people involved in the conflict. So if problems are being raised by the production, technical, or purchasing managers, the quality manager must be on equal terms with them. Some of the more successful companies appoint quality directors.

ACTION SUMMARY

- Do you have a quality system approved to a recognised standard?
- If not, why not?
- Is your quality system a burden, or the basis for a competitive edge?
- What quality improvements has your system delivered?

Answer the above questions, then:

- If you do not have a quality system, start thinking now about implementing BS5750 or the new ISO9000.
- Ensure that all managers understand the reason for the system.
- Educate and train to secure real commitment.
- Make sure that the quality improvement elements of the system are operated.

8 QUALITY COSTS

*You can easily take
some quality costs
for granted and
underestimate your
cost of quality*
Not long ago, a company making large fabrications called
in a consultant to advise on ways in which quality costs
might be reduced. They had obtained BS5750 approval and
were rather proud of this, but it did not seem to be doing
very much to reduce their costs.

They told the consultant that the cost of scrap and
rework was 0.75% of the manufacturing cost, excluding
the cost of process scrap, which is an expense in profiling
large plate. Rather surprised by this information, the
consultant took a walk around the factory. There were
about 100 direct workers, and he found that seven welders
were spending all their time on weld rectification. It does
not require a degree in mathematics to work out that this

alone comes to a lot more than 0.75% of manufacturing costs. The company's response was 'There's always weld rectification – it's part of the process' – so it was not counted as rework.

A closer look at work in the factory revealed that a great deal of weld dressing was being done in order to tidy up the appearance of welds, and that much of this was inside tanks which were going to be filled with oil. The company was also doing a lot of inspection – about 10% of hourly paid employees were inspectors. But this was not counted as a quality cost. These inspectors were considered to be an overhead, charged as a 25% rate on the labour cost.

The moral is that unless extreme care is taken, a distorted idea of the cost of quality may be created, simply because some quality costs are taken for granted and are thus overlooked. Counting these and other concealed inspection costs, the afore-mentioned company eventually agreed that its overall quality cost was in the region of 30% of manufacturing costs, which is typical for a company of its type. As a percentage of sales costs, the average cost of quality in UK manufacturing companies is about 15%.

DETERMINING QUALITY COSTS

How should quality costs be determined? Basic rules for quality costing can be obtained from a British Standard, BS 6143, and a similar guide is published by the American Society for Quality Control. The starting-point is to divide quality costs into four categories:

- Prevention.
- Appraisal.
- Internal failure.
- External failure.

The list can be simplified by talking of 'cost of compliance', which combines the costs of prevention and of appraisal, and 'cost of non-compliance' as the cost of both internal and external failure (Fig. 8.1). We shall however keep to the four headings.

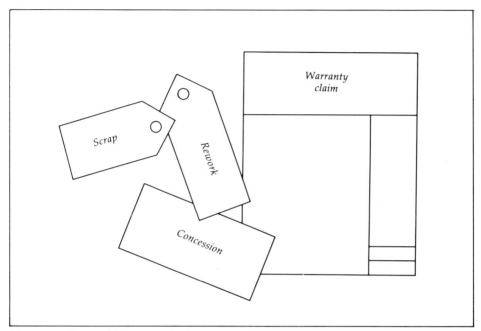

Fig. 8.1. Costs of failure are both internal to the company and external

Cost of prevention is the amount spent to ensure that things are right first time. It includes the cost of making sure that the design is right before anything is made, so activities like design reviews are included. The cost of calibrating equipment is also a prevention cost, as is the whole expense of running a quality assurance system, and the launching and administration of a quality improvement programme.

Cost of appraisal is the sum spent on inspection and testing. It includes all the expenses, including overheads, associated with inspecting and testing the company's own products at every stage of manufacture, as well as the inspection and testing that are carried out on the suppliers' products.

Cost of internal failure is the cost of rectifying everything that is discovered to be wrong while the product or service is still in the company's possession or under its control. All scrap and rework is included under this heading. It also includes, for example, all the costs incurred in obtaining concessions from the design office on sub-standard work.

Cost of external failure is the cost to the business of a product going wrong after it has been handed over to the customer. This may be a very serious item indeed. It includes the cost to the business of providing a bad service which dissuades a customer from coming back or even persuades him or her to cancel a current contract. The cost of warranty and of field service are also included, and even without the impact of product liability legislation, the consequences of having to recall a product for safety or health reasons can lead to the collapse of the company.

A more detailed, though not complete, list of items to be included under the different cost headings is given in Fig. 8.2.

The good news contained in all this is that a cost can be used to cut a cost. The more that is spent on prevention and appraisal, the less the company will have to spend to recover from failures.

Spending money on appraisal (inspection and testing) and money on prevention of bad quality will both reduce your costs of failure, but the two methods work in quite different ways. There is a classical diagram used to illustrate the breakdown of quality costs, a typical version of which is shown in Fig. 8.3. This shows a minimum value for total quality costs at the point at which the rising value of prevention and appraisal costs fails to produce a larger saving in failure costs.

Spending money on prevention will reduce all other quality costs

This is however a misleading conclusion, and explains why we prefer to separate prevention costs from appraisal costs. Spending more on inspection and testing, the main ingredients of appraisal costs, will certainly reduce the amount of defective work getting through to the final product or to the end customer, but it is a method which gives diminishing returns, and beyond a certain point it generates more expense in inspection man-hours than it saves in scrap, rework and warranty.

Prevention work, on the other hand, can continue reducing failure costs almost indefinitely. Companies that

COSTS OF PREVENTION	COSTS OF INTERNAL FAILURE
• Quality engineering	• Scrap
• Design and development of quality measurement and control equipment	• Rework
• Quality planning (functions other than QA)	• Troubleshooting
• Calibration	• Analysis of defects and failures
• Training	• Reinspection and retest
• Administration of QA system (BS5750 procedures)	• Lost production due to supplier material
• System audits	• Lost production due to own material
• Improvement projects	• Modification permits (contrary to process sheets)
COSTS OF APPRAISAL	
• Laboratory acceptance testing	
• Inspection and test	COSTS OF EXTERNAL FAILURE
• Inspection and test set-up	• Complaints administration
• Inspection and test materials	• Product or customer service
• In-process inspection (not by inspectors)	• Product liability
• Product quality audits	• Product returns
• Review of inspection and test results prior to acceptance	• Product recalls
• Evaluation at customers' sites	• Product replacement
• Data processing of inspection and test reports	• Marketing errors

Fig. 8.2. Classification of quality costs

have spent more and more on prevention have always found that their total quality cost has continued to fall. A pioneer company in developing quality cost management is ITT. Recently an ITT quality director, John Hagan, published a paper in which he advised companies not to be too concerned about prevention costs, because these are difficult to measure, and on the whole the higher they are, the better for the company.

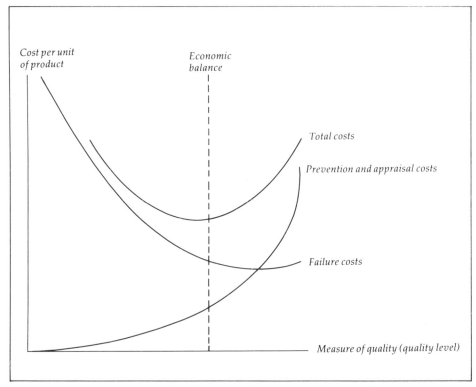

Fig. 8.3.   Classical analysis of quality costs showing a minimum value

A much better model for quality cost control, therefore, is that pictured in Fig. 8.4. Prevention costs, when effectively applied, reduce all other types of quality cost, including appraisal costs, and the result is a continuing reduction in overall quality costs. The key fact is that, for most companies, internal and external failure costs combined far exceed the cost of prevention.

QUALITY COST ALLOCATION

There are some grey areas in quality cost allocation

The lists given in Fig. 8.2 show where most cost items should be allocated, but there are some grey areas which are no so readily classifiable. Plunkett and Dale of UMIST have classified these under four headings:

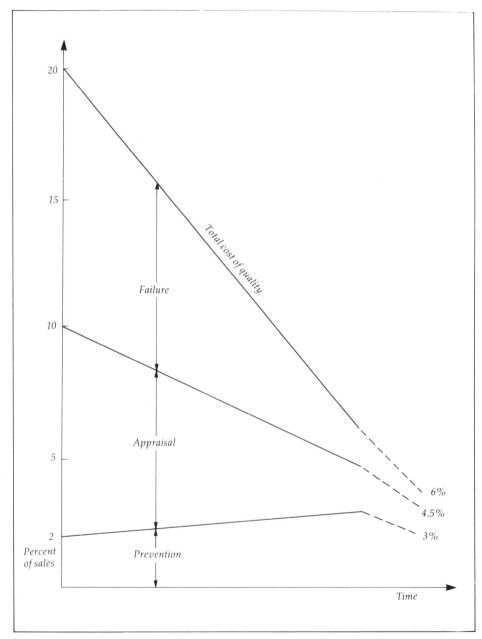

Fig. 8.4.   *Total Quality continuously drives down overall costs by effective use of prevention costs*

- Product test and burn-in.
- Functions other than production.
- Factors basic to the nature of the product.
- Overhead costs.

Product test and burn-in. This could be treated as part of the production process, or as an appraisal cost. For example, if you are making diesel engines you may select some at random for a lengthy running test; and in electronics manufacture it is common practice to burn-in all circuits for a fixed number of hours.

A good way of deciding whether this is part of the process, or an appraisal cost, is to ask how much rework is performed at the end of the test. If no defects or rework are necessary after the test, and the only reason it is being done is to satisfy a customer's requirement, then it is reasonable to treat it as part of the process. In that case, you might try to persuade the customer that it is unnecessary. If on the other hand there is a significant proportion of rejected product at the end, the testing should be considered as an appraisal cost.

Functions other than production. Calculating the cost of quality is an activity which falls in part to the accounts department. It has to isolate the costs of failure by assigning various values, for example to scrap notes. This is a difficult exercise which may not at first be seen by the accounts people as being particularly useful. Should it be charged as a quality appraisal cost? Similarly, the purchasing department may spend considerable time analysing the performance of suppliers to decide which are the most reliable ones. Is this to be counted as a prevention cost, or is it simply part of the purchasing function? In any case, you must consider what benefit will be gained from trying to analyse the time spent in dealing with matters such as reject notes to suppliers, credit notes and so on.

Factors basic to the nature of the product. In process industries, particularly, virtually every activity is concerned with obtaining optimum yields and meeting specifications, so that everything could theoretically be classified as a quality cost, and in most cases as a cost of prevention.

Service industries are in a similar situation. If you are handling insurance claims, or providing counter service in a bank, how can 'quality' activities be separated from simply doing the job? In some occupations quality is intrinsic to the requirements of the job: for example, a nurse in a maternity ward cannot be given an 'acceptable quality level' of 1%, allowing her or him to drop 1% of babies.

Overhead costs. We have mentioned the overheads of the inspection department, but the way in which overheads are allocated can inflate the cost of appraisal or of scrap and rework out of all proportion to other costs, and in particular out of proportion to any opportunity to recover those costs in the short term as a result of a campaign of quality improvement.

RESOLVING GREY AREAS IN QUALITY

How the grey areas are dealt with depends on what the information is needed for

How should these grey areas be resolved? This problem is not unique to quality costs: it crops up in any costing exercise. The way you tackle it depends on what you want the information for, which is the next key question to be considered.

There are four different but perfectly valid reasons for which you may wish to carry out a quality cost analysis:

- To shock people into action.
- To provide a basis for an improvement programme.
- To monitor improvements during a programme.
- To make comparisons with another division of the company.

Each of these aims will lead to a different method of analysing quality costs (Fig. 8.5).

If you are trying to *shock people into taking action* to change quality costs, you should compare the present situation with an ultimate target level in which failure costs and appraisal costs have been reduced to zero in a new

* *Shock into action*
  * *what could the operation be like with no failure or appraisal?*
  * *compare present situation with possible greenfield site*
  * *include all overheads even if change cannot affect them in short-to-medium term*

* *Provide a basis for improvement*
  * *include only those costs where measurable reductions can be obtained in the short-to-medium term; emphasis is on opportunities for real savings*

* *Monitor improvement projects*
  * *continue measurement system through project life: basis must be consistent through time; costs measured must be controllable; cost collection must be accurate, economic and timely*

* *Compare with other division*
  * *basis of cost collection must be consistent, unambiguous and accepted*

Fig. 8.5.   Purpose of the project determines the method of analysing quality costs

factory on a greenfield site. In this situation you will want to include all quality-related overheads, even if nothing can be done about them in the short or medium term.

For example, you may find that 10% of production is being lost in scrap and rework. Because of the state of business, it might not be possible in practice to increase sales by 10% if that waste were to be eliminated. It *would* be theoretically possible, though, to carry on the same level of business using 10% less people, supervision, floor area, power, heat, light and so on. It is unlikely that you could move into a building with 10% less floor area, cut your supervisory staff by just 10% and so on as an immediate consequence of eliminating scrap and rework, but you can quite reasonably assume this when you are making a quick calculation of potential quality cost savings for presentation to company management.

This approach is useful in obtaining a first estimate of quality costs, in order to get some idea of the scale of problems and opportunities. You can use BS6143 as a basis, without bothering too much about accuracy. It should not take more than a few days to build up a broad picture of the distribution of different types of quality costs in the company.

If as a result of this preliminary exercise, the company decides that something must be done about quality improvement, a more precise analysis is needed to highlight cost areas where real improvements can be made in the short to medium term. In this case every item of quality cost must be studied to identify what could actually be saved by eliminating it. Preparing the company for this more detailed study may entail running a training programme to ensure that people understand the aims and can identify the quality cost issues.

For example, if you have an automatic machine which is producing a scrap rate of 10% and has an overhead charge rate of £20 an hour, if changes were made to eliminate the production of scrap, you might not be able to use the extra production capability. In that case you could not expect to save the full 10% of £20 an hour. However, the machine can be switched off for that unused 10% of its time, with a consequent saving of power, consumables, and wear and tear. Also saved will be the time of the inspector, who will no longer have to sort the good from the bad. The final savings estimate will not be as high as it would be using the first method above, but it will be more useful in calculating potential savings and in deciding where you should concentrate your efforts.

Costing the progress of improvement projects must only include items controllable by the staff concerned

Having obtained figures to provide a foundation for improvements, you will want to set up improvement projects to ensure that the changes take place. The requirements for a quality cost system to monitor projects will be slightly different again. You will have to continue taking measurements throughout the life of the project, and therefore the basis of measurement must remain constant so that progress can be charted accurately.

If the method of charging overhead rates is altered during the course of a project, it can completely overwhelm any quality cost improvements that have been achieved.

Quality costs used for monitoring a project must be controllable by the people responsible for that project.

The standard overhead rate charged to a production shop may well include an allowance for rent and rates on the space occupied, even though the shop manager can do nothing to control them. If the local council increases the rates, the company cost accountants will pass on the expense as an additional overhead charge on the factory, with the result that, just as the shop manager is about to congratulate his quality improvement team on its highly successful performance, the figures arrive, showing a massive increase in quality costs. This is no way to encourage a quality improvement programme. The absolute rule is therefore that cost monitoring for an improvement programme must include only those factors which can be controlled by the group.

As with any costing system, quality cost monitoring must not itself cost more than is going to be saved by the improvement project. It must be timely. It must be available with a frequency appropriate to the kind of action being taken in the project. If you expect to see changes on a weekly basis, you should have the cost information on a weekly basis: it is useless if you have to wait months for it.

Inter-plant comparisons are useful, provided a fair basis for comparison can be found

The fourth type of cost exercise is to make comparisons between different factories or divisions in a large or medium-sized company. It is in practice exceedingly difficult to find factories which are sufficiently alike for people to accept that there is a fair basis for comparison. There are many different cost elements which must be interpreted consistently between the divisions to be compared. Definitions must be completely unambiguous, and there is no point in attempting a comparison unless the people concerned accept its basis.

THE TAGUCHI VIEW OF QUALITY COSTS

What we have just described represents the classical approach to quality costs. There is however a growing

Lack of quality as a loss to society: Taguchi's view

interest today in a radically different way of looking at the cost of quality, a method which has been introduced by the Japanese quality expert Dr Genichi Taguchi, whose approach to design for quality is reviewed in Chapter 12.

Taguchi defines the quality of a product in a negative sense as 'the loss imparted by the product to society from the time the product is shipped'. There is a loss to society associated with every product, and the aim of its manufacturer must be to minimise such loss. Taguchi views this loss in the broadest terms. It can obviously include such things as air pollution from a defective motor car exhaust, inefficiency in the functioning of a pump and so on, but Taguchi would also include all kinds of dissatisfaction to the consumer, as well as warranty costs to the producer and lost business resulting from a poor reputation.

Any variation from the optimum imparts a loss to society

It should be remembered that we are concerned now with the sophisticated world of Japanese industry, where crude quality costs of prevention, appraisal and failure are under control, and the focus of attention has shifted to the design of the product. Taguchi argues that any departure from a specified target value imparts a loss. One example he takes is the AC-DC converting circuit used in a television set, where (in Japan) the AC input is 110 volts, and the DC output is set at 115 volts. This is its target value, and tolerance limits of, say ±15 volts may be set on it. However, if you have the choice of taking converters from a factory which is supplying them within the 15-volt limits, or from a factory which is supplying them within 8-volt limits, you will choose the latter, other things being equal.

Taguchi uses this example to underline his point that any variation from the target value incurs a loss, and that this loss becomes greater the more the product deviates from its target value. He has found in practice that the loss frequently approximates to the parabolic form shown in Fig. 8.6, which he calls the quadratic loss function.

This leads on to an important argument which highlights the importance of conforming as closely as possible to the optimum rather than being content with remaining inside

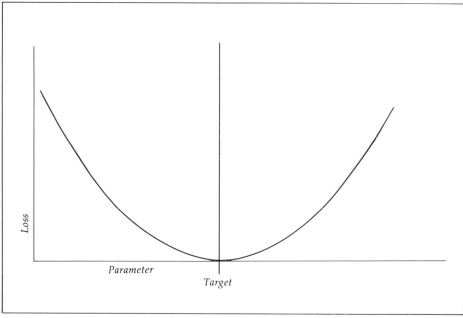

Fig. 8.6.   Taguchi's quadratic loss function. Any departure from target value of a parameter involves a loss to society

Even conforming to specification is more costly than hitting the exact target
'acceptable' specification limits. If a manufacturing process is not capable of turning out products entirely within specification, but all defective products are intercepted and removed by inspection, the distribution of 'acceptable' products will be something like that shown in Fig. 8.7. By contrast a process which is statistically capable will have a distribution like that shown superimposed on the first distribution in Fig. 8.8. Even though a few parts from the capable process may be outside the specification limits, the great majority will be closer to the target value than with the other process, with the result that the overall loss to society, based on Taguchi's quadratic loss function, is much less.

Customers want to minimise their total costs, not just the product price
Quality is primarily concerned with reducing variability. This is far more important than simply being within specification, as can be seen from the Taguchi diagrams. It may be thought that the 'cost to society' is a fastidious notion in the tough, competitive world of industry, but it

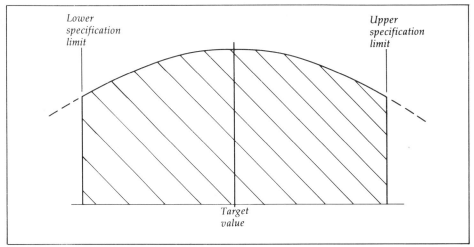

Fig. 8.7. Distribution of parts from an incapable process but with those outside specification limits removed

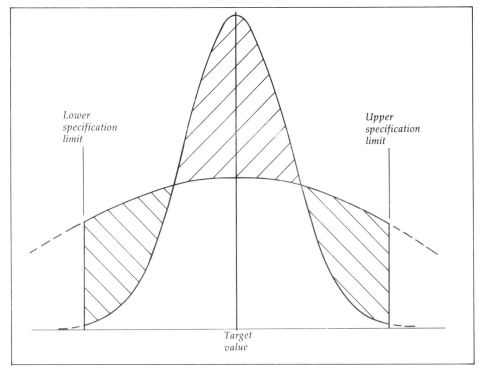

Fig. 8.8. Comparison with capable process – ± 3σ within specification limits

must be considered from the viewpoint of the customers. Their concern is to minimise their overall costs, not simply the short-term price of the goods they are buying.

Taguchi quotes the case of a manufacturer of vinyl sheeting for agricultural use on cloches. The manufacturer found he was able to reduce his process variability by 90%, so that instead of producing to a thickness tolerance of ± 0.2mm he could keep within ± 0.02mm. To minimise his costs he therefore adjusted the average thickness (in statistical language, the process mean) down to the bottom end of the range accepted in his specification. The result was that the vinyl sheet became much more prone to tearing, and resulted in heavy losses to the farmers in damaged crops. For the relatively small saving made by the manufacturer, there was a much greater loss to society as a whole, and to the farmers in particular.

Taguchi describes such action by a manufacturer as "more immoral than the actions of a thief", because when the thief steals 10,000 Yen the victim loses 10,000 Yen and society is no worse off. But a manufacturer who moves his or her process mean to the bottom of the specification range imposes a much larger loss – say 20,000 Yen – on his or her customers so that he or she can make a 10,000 Yen profit. By ignoring Taguchi's principle you may in the short term make more money, but in the longer term you will lose your reputation and business to other companies who take the principle seriously.

ACTION SUMMARY

- Estimate the cost of quality to your business under the headings: prevention, appraisal, internal failure, and external failure.
- Identify the major opportunities for cost reduction.
- Plan actions to take the opportunities, while recognising that prevention costs may increase.
- Carry out the plans.
- Ensure that cost reductions have been achieved.
- Examine the total loss imparted to society by your product. Could this be reduced?

9 WORKING WITH SUPPLIERS

Expect your suppliers to have a policy of Total Quality

Picture, if you can, an ideal supplier, and imagine what his or her virtues would be. A short list might include the following:

- Products that are always 100% correct and reliable.
- Deliveries that are always on time.
- Quantities that are delivered are always correct: there are never too few or too many items.
- Deliveries that occur daily to minimise the stock carried by the user.
- The supplier is willing to accept changes in the quantities ordered, even up to a day before delivery.
- If something does go wrong, there is total commitment to righting it again as rapidly as possible.
- Competitive product pricing.

The theme of this book is that anything short of perfection must be challenged. If you have accepted this philosophy in your own operations and in the service you offer to your customers, it is reasonable to expect it of your suppliers. More than that, it is essential, because you cannot give your customers the service they expect of you unless you in turn can rely on your suppliers.

ACHIEVING COLLABORATION

Mutual trust and collaboration with your suppliers are the first essential

How do you set about achieving such a relationship? In the first place, you will certainly not achieve it by taking an adversarial attitude to your suppliers – the stance adopted by purchasing managers whose primary aim is to bargain for the lowest possible price. The first essential is to build a relationship of mutual trust and collaboration.

When you are looking for a supplier for a particular product, what you are really buying is not simply the product itself, but also the capabilities of the supplier, and in this context more important than anything else (more important, even, than the supplier's present ability to meet your technical specification) is the commitment to meeting your requirements in terms of both quality and delivery. If you find a company with a corporate strategy, or a small businessman with a business philosophy, which puts service to the customer as the primary aim, then it may be worthwhile to do business, even though currently there may be some technical limitations which will require your help if the supplier is to overcome them.

This is an approach to supplier relationships which has been pioneered by firms such as Marks and Spencer, and which is also found in some automotive companies. A company supplying air filters and cleaner bodies to Volvo was having difficulties with the air filters, which were running at a reject rate of 20%. The company was approached by Volvo engineers, whose concerns were whether it had the technical know-how to solve the problem and whether there was any support which Volvo could give in solving it. Volvo knew that the company was committed to providing the quality and delivery service required of it, and was thus prepared to help the company improve and then sustain acceptable standards.

Study your supplier's management and employee relations

Study the management team of a potential supplier. Are they hungry for your business? Are they prepared to commit themselves to do everything in their power to make your business successful? Are they willing to open up their business to you so that you can collaborate closely on quality improvement – to the extent also of giving access to *their* suppliers?

Look at the company's employee relations. Does it have a good history of industrial relations? Can you be confident of continuity of supply? Is there a positive attitude towards quality at all levels in the company? If there is, and it is reinforced by quality circles or improvement groups, this will give added confidence that the company will have your interests at heart.

A commitment to Total Quality on the part of your supplier is something to look for, and you may require some formal certification such as approval to BS5750, or evidence of approval by a major quality-conscious customer. BS5750 approval ensures that a company has the organisation necessary to give assurance of quality to its customers, although, as we have seen, this in itself is not a guarantee that the company fully appreciates the principles underlying the standard.

Look for a commitment to continuous quality improvement

The technical competence of the company to supply your needs is an obvious requirement. When you accept Taguchi's approach, you should also look for a willingness to continue development activities, and, where appropriate, to invest in new plant in order to go on raising levels of performance and quality in the future.

Do the company's products and services meet your technical requirements? Does the company have the capacity to accommodate extra work if demand for your products increases in future, and is there the ability and willingness to increase capacity if necessary?

In present market conditions, where stocks and work in progress must be kept to a minimum, you may also decide

Total Quality and Just-in-time support each other that you must organise your manufacturing on a Just-in-time (JIT) basis. In that case you will need your supplier to deliver on a regular – perhaps daily or twice-daily – basis to avoid your having to hold stocks of goods awaiting production. Automobile and food manufacturing industries routinely work on this basis, for reasons of space or perishability, but there is also a powerful incentive towards JIT in terms of the inventory cost savings it offers.

If you are serving a consumer goods market, the conditions imposed on you may require changes at extremely short notice in the types and quantities of goods you dispatch. For your own survival you will need to impose similar conditions on your suppliers. This requirement in turn feeds back into the need for adoption of Total Quality by your supplier, because any defects in goods supplied to you will have an immediate impact on your operations.

Be wary of suppliers that are much larger than your own company The size of your supplier's organisation can be an important factor. If your contracts add up to only a tiny proportion of your supplier's total business, you will not be in a strong position to take advantage of quality improvement opportunities such as those we have been discussing. Rather than doing business directly with, say, a major steel manufacturer, your company may well get better service from a stockholder to whom your company's account is important and who will go to great pains to ensure continuity and quality of supply. A good stockholder will use his or her superior purchasing power to gain access to alternative sources of supply in order to maintain quality.

For example, a food manufacturing company needed for its product a dark-brown sugar of a particular colour, which it was accustomed to buying from one of the major suppliers. There were frequent troubles and arguments because deliveries were not consistently of the correct colour, resulting in loss of production and of management time. The user's business was not large enough to be of great significance to the supplier.

Eventually, the company opted to buy its sugar from an intermediary, who selected the bags of the required colour and sold the others to other customers for whom the colour was not critical. The sugar cost a little more, but this was more than paid for by the savings created by the reduced stockholding, the continuity of production, the saving in management time, and the fact that it was no longer necessary to employ somebody to check every bag as it came in, using expensive colorimetric equipment.

SINGLE-SOURCE PURCHASING

Single-source purchasing is the logical consequence of Total Quality

The logical consequence of making such demands on your supplier is that you will adopt a policy of single sourcing for each purchased product line. This is the approach increasingly adopted by companies which have made a commitment to Total Quality. The advantages are obvious:

- You get a better service. A supplier who has all your business for a particular product will be better able to invest in its present and future quality. You will also be in a stronger position to expect the best service from him or her.
- You reduce the amount of monitoring of the purchased product.
- You can develop a close collaborative relationship with your supplier, in which each party sees it as in his or her interest to support the other.
- You can get a better price. If you are spreading your widget business over three suppliers, each has a relatively small proportion of your business, so that his or her unit costs are much higher than if he or she supplied all your widgets.

Single-source resource management is always the objective to be aimed for. If you cannot find a supplier prepared to make the sort of commitment described, your risk is greater. It may still be best for you to keep to a single supplier for the product, but you will have to commit yourself to a more comprehensive programme of goods inward inspection. Goods inward inspection is necessary for any new supplier, but as you gain confidence in him or her and can rely on his or her ability to deliver only products within your specification, you can reduce your inspection to the minimum level of sampling, simply to verify that his or her processes are under control.

Structural changes in your organisation can follow a policy of single sourcing

Where the responsibility for quality has been firmly taken by your suppliers, the structure of your company's quality and purchasing organisations can be substantially different. More senior management time should be devoted to making sure the relationship with the supplier is right, and less inspection time should be devoted to making sure that an unprincipled supplier is not trying to unload poor work on you.

In the purchasing department, the emphasis shifts to minimising the cost of purchase by eliminating the expense of incoming goods inspection, the sorting of faulty batches, lost production due to incoming goods being late or rejected, and fluctuating raw material quality levels. Overall, therefore, the parochial concern to minimise purchasing spending at any cost is replaced by ensuring excellence of supply at minimum practicable cost.

Single sourcing does not remove the need for the traditional purchasing skills, such as vigilance in ensuring that the supplier is still offering the best value for money in the market-place, taking into account all the relevant factors. You still need to look at your suppliers' competition, at their prices, their quality and the service they can offer, and to test samples from them alongside current products. But more time should be spent in building successful collaboration than in trying to shave a little off prices. If you continue to push a supplier to reduce prices, he or she is liable to maintain his or her profit by paying less attention to quality, and you will be the loser in the long run.

To give a taste of the collaboration which can be achieved within a framework of single sourcing and Total Quality, we offer this true account of the experience of a food manufacturing company.

The company was supplying chilled cooked foods to a major retailer at the rate of about four million portions a year. The business was characterised by very short lead times: the customer indicated requirements three days ahead, but could, and often would, change the order as little as 24 hours before delivery. The production cycle was about 16 hours. Production started at about 4 p.m., and everything was packed and ready to be taken by special chilled transport by 9 a.m. next morning.

The particular product discussed here was duck à l'orange, which is a quarter roast duckling with orange sauce and fresh orange segments. The ingredients were bought from outside suppliers and came in fresh, only four to six hours before manufacturing began, and there was, by design, only limited space for holding chilled ingredients. The making of stock for the sauce began at 4 p.m. Duckling were roasted overnight, starting at 10 p.m. Fresh oranges were prepared and added, starting at 7 a.m. The duckling were boned and cut and the complete meals were packed ready for dispatch starting from 9 a.m.

A quality problem was encountered at 9.30 one morning when a ring of fat was discovered around the sauce. Knowing that it would not be acceptable to the customer, the consignment was rejected. The supplier of ducklings was informed immediately, a sample was sent to the customer, and an internal audit was begun on the quality control records for the suspect batch, to check whether any procedures had been followed incorrectly. At 4 p.m. the managing director of the supplier of ducklings was on-site for cooking trials, and he did not leave until midnight.

By 8 o'clock the next morning the general manager and technical manager had taken samples of the night's production to the supplier, and possible causes for the trouble were reviewed. The technical manager went on with the supplier's managing director to see the nutritionist of his feed supplier, while the general manager went to report to the customer. At 6 p.m. they were back on-site for the next cooking trials.

At 8 a.m. on the third day, representatives of the customer, the supplier and his feed supplier met, and within two hours had reached an agreement on the feed specification, since this turned out to be the cause of the trouble. The same afternoon, the technical manager went to see the breeder of the ducklings to discuss alternative breeds.

It took just three days to discover and deal with the cause of the trouble, but this was only possible because of the complete commitment of all the parties concerned to Total Quality. Another supplier might well have temporised and suggested carrying out another cooking trial, which would have wasted at least one more day. This supplier accepted immediately that the trouble might have something to do with his products, and not only offered immediate help, but also gave direct access to his feed supplier, which helped considerably in quickly identifying the root cause of the trouble. Needless to say, all the companies concerned operated a policy of single sourcing.

ACTION SUMMARY

- How many sources do you have for key supplies, and why?
- Identify the best sources, based on quality, delivery and commitment.
- Set targets for your buyers, based on quality and delivery.
- Reduce your sources to the minimum.
- Phase out receiving inspection as you establish trust with suppliers.

TECHNOLOGY

This section of the book concerns the technology of Total Quality. It must be emphasised immediately that this is not an 'optional extra'. Statistical methods, in particular, are essential to the continuous reduction of variance which is the central theme of this book. If you are unable to work with statistical tools, you cannot implement Total Quality.

It is not our purpose to write a textbook on metrology or statistics – there are plenty of books available on both subjects – but we wish to underline the fact that it is just as important to understand and use the technological tools of Total Quality as it is to have a highly motivated workforce and a good quality management structure. These three chapters aim to provide a clear introduction, in non-technical language, to the key concepts which are essential to a quality improvement programme. If your interest is in the overall management of a quality programme, these chapters will provide you with the language for communicating with the specialists. If you intend to become more deeply involved, we hope at least to give you an overview from which to start.

The section begins with a review of the role of measurement in quality, and progresses to the interpretation of data by using statistics, and to an introduction to some more advanced techniques, including the parameter design methods of the Japanese expert, Genichi Taguchi.

10 METROLOGY

Precise standards of measurement are fundamental to an integrated industrial society

Measurement is an element fundamental to human civilisation. Without at least some basic forms of measurement, it would be impossible to build a house, make a table or bake a cake. To design and build an aeroplane, or a machine for making paper-clips, or to make the raw material for a plastic washing-up bowl, demands measurement of a much higher order. It also demands something much more complicated and difficult to achieve: *standards* of measurement.

A craftsman making a table can work by eye and with the simplest measuring devices. He or she can make sure the legs are the same length by placing them together, and can mark out an accurate joint with the help of a try-square and a marking gauge. It is not essential to fix the precise size. But if he or she is going into production of batches of identical tables, when it comes to buying his or her materials by the metre, kilogramme or other assorted units currently in use, he or she will be thankful for closely defined standards of measurement.

Standards of measurement for length, weight, capacity and so on have a long history. They are found in the earliest written documents from Egypt and Mesopotamia. The motive at that time seems to have been largely pecuniary: people wanted to know just how much olive oil they were getting for their carefully weighed gold coins, and whether they would get a better bargain from the next farmer down the road. The word 'geometry' is derived from a Greek word for the measurement of land, so the work of Pythagoras was not only of philosophical interest.

The present-day role of standards as the foundation of interchangeable manufacturing and the use of subcontractors is of much more recent origin, and can probably be dated to the development of the railways. Suddenly it became possible and economical to send both semi-finished products and finished components and assemblies around the country. Firms were able to concentrate their efforts on more restricted product ranges, and there developed an urgent need for standards, both to ensure higher precision of measurement and to establish agreement on such basic products as screw threads. Small wonder, then, that Sir Joseph Whitworth, who developed his standard screw thread in 1839, remains famous to this day.

All measuring equipment depends on a calibration chain that links it back to international standards

Precise standards of measurement – not only of dimensions but of weight, temperature, pressure, voltage, current and many other quantities – are fundamental to an integrated industrial society in which a microcomputer designed in the USA and assembled in the UK may use a case moulded in West Germany, a monitor tube from Holland and electronic components from all over the Far East. For this to be possible, every measuring device in every company must be calibrated, so that each metre rule is the same length.

The way this uniformity is achieved throughout the country and the world is through a calibration chain which can be traced back to a single set of international standards. Each country has its own national set of standards, and these are regularly calibrated against international standards to ensure that they all agree with each other.

Within the UK, the national standards are held and maintained by the National Physical Laboratory (NPL) at Teddington, Middlesex, and the calibration of every measuring device used in British industry should be traceable back to the NPL standards. This does not necessarily mean that every multimeter in use must be sent regularly to Teddington for recalibration. It is more likely that it will be checked regularly against a company standard which is kept purely for reference purposes and is carefully protected to preserve it from deterioration.

The company reference standard may be sent periodically to Teddington, or it may go to an approved calibration centre which in turn will send its reference standards to Teddington. At the NPL, measuring equipment which is sent for calibration is checked not against the national reference standards, but against a set of 'transfer standards', which in turn are calibrated against the national reference standards. When the newly calibrated set of reference standards comes back to the company, they will be used to calibrate transfer standards for regular calibration use, and the reference standards will be kept locked away in a clean dry cupboard and rarely used.

For some types of measurement, there can be a short cut to avoid this lengthy calibration chain, by calibrating against a physical constant such as the wavelength of light of a particular colour, and some users may find that the expense of such specialist equipment is justified. In general, though, *the calibration chain with traceable links leading back to international standards is vital to present-day manufacturing.*

IMPLICATIONS OF THE CALIBRATION CHAIN

Interchangeable manufacture within and between companies depends on the calibration chain

A skilled toolmaker working alone at a bench, with his or her own micrometer, can work within tolerances of less than one-hundredth of a millimetre, and can produce extremely fine fits. Even in the eighteenth century, the clockmakers of London could work individually to very exacting tolerances, but could not interchange parts between different clocks. Equally, today's toolmaker, unless his or her micrometer is regularly calibrated, and he or she uses the ratchet device on the micrometer to give constant pressure, will not produce work which is interchangeable with other people's, however accurate the fits he or she can produce individually.

James Watt is famous for being the first person to design and build efficient steam engines, but he trained as an instrument-maker in London. To try out his ideas for a self-condensing steam engine, he built a bench prototype while working as instrument-maker to Glasgow University. It proved remarkably powerful. But when he had a larger engine built by Carron Iron Works, requiring the co-operation of a team of craftsmen, it would not run at all, because the clearance between piston and cylinder was big enough for him to put his hand through.

Each link in the calibration chain introduces a degree of error

Ensuring that all your measuring equipment is linked to the calibration chain is therefore the first essential, which is why so much stress is laid upon the subject in documents such as BS5750. The next important consideration to be aware of is that each link in the calibration chain introduces a degree of error.

If the same item – a length, a weight, a voltage – is measured ten times with the same piece of equipment, the same result will not be obtained every time. There will be a small amount of variation between readings, arising partly from slight variations in the way the measurement was made, and partly from small inaccuracies in the measuring equipment. However, unless there were special factors affecting some of the readings, all the measurements will tend to cluster around a central value, and if a large number of readings are taken, they will be seen to form a pattern like that shown in Fig. 10.1. This is called a normal distribution, and will be discussed further in Chapter 11.

The normal distribution is a powerful aid to the quality engineer, because not only do most types of measurements follow this pattern, but by measuring the scatter in a sample of ten readings, the amount of scatter there will be in future readings can be confidently predicted. A number can even be put on the proportion of future readings which will fall within a certain tolerance band. Alternatively, it can be estimated how wide a tolerance band must be set to ensure that 95% of measurements are contained within it.

If a voltmeter is sent away to the NPL for calibration, it will come back with a report which details the amount of uncertainty that must be expected in its readings: for

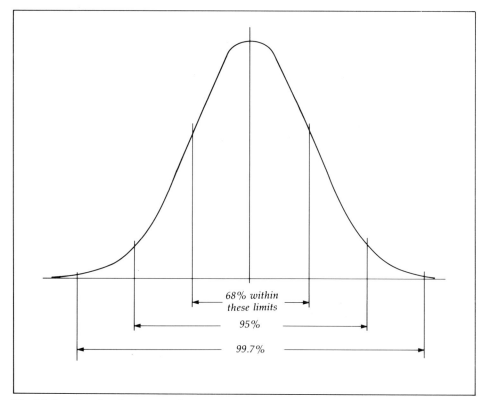

Fig. 10.1. Randomly scattered measurements tend to follow this normal distribution

example, that a reading of 10V could really mean anything from 9.98 to 10.02V.

If this voltmeter is then used as a transfer standard to calibrate the company's shop-floor voltmeters, a new level of uncertainty is introduced. The uncertainty inherent in the transfer standard voltmeter and the uncertainty in the shop-floor instrument will have to be added together.

When the shop-floor instrument in turn is used to measure, say, the power supply for a television set, a further uncertainty will be introduced. Typically, each link in the calibration chain adds one order of magnitude to the uncertainty of measurement – it multiplies the measurement tolerance band ten times. A piece of electrical equipment used on the shop-floor has typically a measuring uncertainty of 1%-2% of its maximum scale reading.

Mechanical engineering companies habitually overestimate their ability to measure accurately

It is important to know the measurement capability of your company's equipment. In our experience, the electrical and electronics industries and the food industry have a pretty good idea of the accuracy of their instrumentation. Unfortunately this is not true of the mechanical engineering industry. Three surveys carried out in the past 30 years have shown that throughout the British mechanical engineering industry, people regularly overestimate their ability to measure accurately by a factor of 10.

One possible reason for this is that many production engineering managers and supervisors started their careers as toolmakers who, as we have seen, can produce highly consistent results when working on their own, but may not be aware of the pitfalls of the calibration chain when making absolute measurements.

Be heedful of the uncertainty of measuring equipment

How can you decide whether a particular instrument is suitable for carrying out a measurement? Some general guidelines on the measuring capability of a number of types of instruments are given in Fig. 10.2. There is a simple rule of thumb that the uncertainty of measurement of your instrument should not be more than one-tenth of the allowable tolerance in whatever it is you are measuring.

Thus, if you are measuring a voltage which is required to be 100V ± 1V, your voltmeter should not have an uncertainty of more than ± 0.1V at that level. The transfer standard voltmeter used to calibrate it should also have an uncertainty of no more than ± 0.01V.

In practice, it may not be possible to achieve a full order of magnitude difference between the uncertainty of the instrument and the allowable tolerance, but it would be dangerous to allow the uncertainty to be more than 20% of the tolerance. You, being a quality-conscious reader, should never allow yourself to get in the situation of one machinist, who was trying to turn an outside diameter of 340mm within a tolerance of 17μm, when the only measuring instrument he had was an ordinary micrometer – which at that diameter must have had a calibration uncertainty in the region of 40μm.

A similar problem arose in another company, where a 300mm-internal diameter light-alloy nuclear reactor cover had a 40μm tolerance. The problem was solved by flood-cooling the component during machining, using coolant which was being continuously refrigerated at 20°C, and keeping the newly calibrated internal micrometer immersed in the coolant tank. The machine was also surrounded by screens to keep it out of draughts. Nothing less than that sort of attention to detail, besides using sufficiently accurate measuring equipment, can produce work to such a level of accuracy.

Uncertainty of measurement is itself built up from three distinct elements:

- Repeatability.
- Reproducibility.
- Calibration errors.

Repeatability of a measurement is 'the agreement between the results of successive measurements of the same value in the same quantity by the same method and the same observer with the same instrument in the same location at short intervals of time'. In other words, it is the result obtained when one observer sits at a bench and with

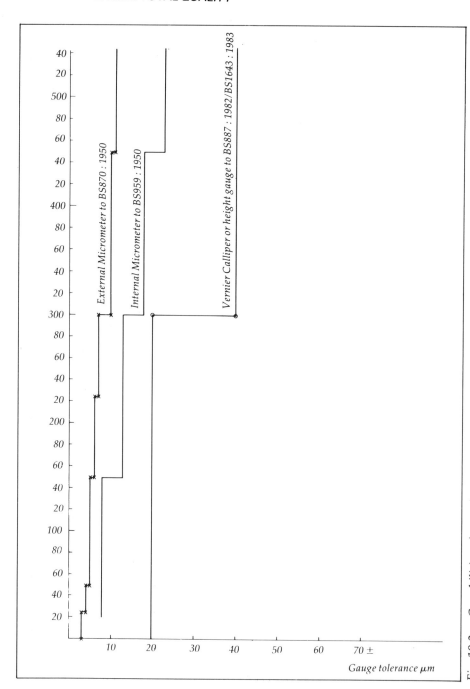

Fig. 10.2.   Capabilities of some frequently used measuring instruments

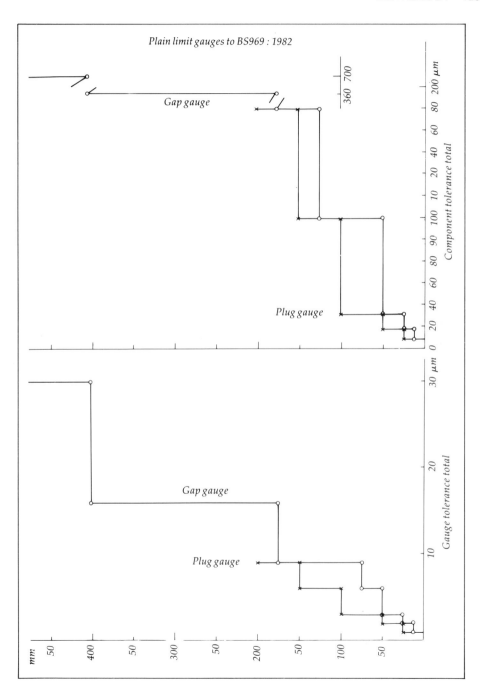

Plain limit gauges to BS969 : 1982

one set of kit takes ten measurements in succession of the same object.

Reproducibility is 'the agreement between results of measurements of the same value in the same quantity where the individual measurements are made under different defined conditions' – so different methods may be used by different people in different places at different times.

The *calibration error* of an instrument is the cumulative total of all the repeatability errors acquired in the course of the calibration chain. When the instrument is used for measurement on the shop-floor, it is also subject to errors of reproducibility, because it will be used in different situations by different people at different times. In practice, with most measuring equipment, the errors of reproducibility are small compared with the calibration errors resulting from lack of repeatability along the calibration chain.

HOW TO CONTROL CALIBRATION

How can you ensure that all equipment is duly calibrated, that the right equipment is being used, and that the errors accumulating from all sources are minimised? This is a good example of the need for the threefold approach to quality, through people, structure and technology. There is no substitute for training. People must be trained to understand the technology – to know the capabilities of different types of instruments, and to appreciate the need for regular calibration; and there must be a system to ensure that the training is done, that the calibration takes place, and so on.

The first step in controlling calibration is to identify every piece of measuring and inspecting equipment in the company, including items such as jigs and fixtures which determine the accuracy of work made with their help. This should also include machine tools, and particularly CNC machines, where the accuracy of scales and slideways determines the accuracy of parts made on them. The equipment should be numbered and indexed, and a decision taken as to how often it should be calibrated.

The decision about frequency of calibration can be refined with experience. The rule is that calibration should be done often enough for a trend to be plotted. The trend line will reveal when the next calibration must take place if the instrument is not to go outside its acceptable limits.

The resources needed for calibration depend on the types of instrumentation in use. Electronic equipment can be calibrated fairly easily, because it is not usually very sensitive to temperature. All that is needed is a reasonably clean working area, the instruments used for carrying out the calibration, a filing cabinet for calibration records and a place to lock up and secure equipment which has been calibrated and found defective. The high-cost items are the calibration instruments, and these will in turn need to be sent away regularly for calibration.

Dimensional measurement is more difficult, because dimensions change when the temperature changes. Calibration therefore needs to be done under reasonably stable temperature conditions. In the factory, it is usually arranged where possible for the measuring instrument to be made of the same material as the product being measured, so that small temperature variations will not matter. In the calibration laboratory, there must be stricter rules, because, as we have seen, accuracy needs to be ten times higher than on the shop-floor. Thermal expansion coefficients vary even between different types of steel and of cast iron, so an air-conditioned laboratory may well be necessary.

The equipment used for dimensional calibration may be quite simple. Most types of engineering calibration can be done with a set of gauge blocks and a comparator, but the procedures can be very slow, and a firm doing much calibration will need to buy more sophisticated equipment. Calibration is a complicated process, and some of the simplest pieces of equipment prove to be the hardest to calibrate – there are, for example, about 20 different steps to be taken in calibrating a basic micrometer.

Written calibration procedures are required by quality assurance standards such as BS5750. In any case they are essential to ensure that the methods are fully and consistently used. Written calibration records are needed to detect any adverse trends in the instruments. Companies are often surprised to discover how many different types of measuring equipment they have, when they start to set up calibration procedures. It is not simply a matter of dealing with dimensional measurement equipment. Torque wrenches, pressure gauges, temperature gauges, electrical and many other types of equipment all need regular calibration with written records.

Most companies find it best to use an outside calibration laboratory

The task of setting up an effective calibration system is highly demanding, and for a small or medium-sized company which does not have a large number of instruments to be calibrated, it is well worth considering the use of an outside calibration laboratory which is accredited by the National Measurement Accreditation Service (NAMAS). This service was formed recently by the amalgamation of the British Calibration Service (BCS) and the National Testing Laboratory Accreditation Scheme. It is operated by the National Physical Laboratory, which maintains surveillance of the laboratories within the scheme. The variety of available calibration links back to NPL is indicated in Fig. 10.3. There is also an international dimension to the service, because NAMAS takes part in the International Laboratory Accreditation Conference, which aims to harmonise criteria and procedures as a means of dismantling technical barriers to trade. BCS calibration certificates are recognised in several European countries and in the USA.

Calibration of machine tools is often overlooked, though the accuracy of work produced on them depends on their measuring capability. Precision machines are often kept running in factories for five or ten years without any check on their accuracy, which will inevitably deteriorate over time. The axes of motion lose straightness, and, even more important, the geometrical relationships between the machine axes move out of true.

There is a set of British Standards, BS4656, relating to

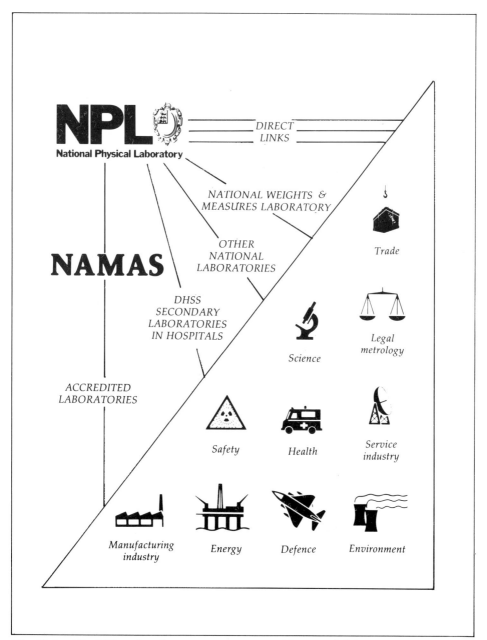

Fig. 10.3. The UK national measurement system (Courtesy of the National Physical Laboratory, UK)

the calibration of machine tools, and equipment can be bought to enable companies to do their own calibration. However, it is expensive, and unless the number of machines is large and the demands on accuracy are extremely strict, it is better to subcontract the work to a specialist company, which will also calibrate your coordinate measuring machines.

ACTION SUMMARY

- Review available measurement and test equipment against product specification limits.
- Ensure that all measurement and test equipment is calibrated.
- Ensure that all production equipment is calibrated.

11 THE ROLE OF STATISTICS

Japanese manufacturing quality is founded on technology

Japan watchers who have been pointing out in recent years the strong Japanese emphasis on quality, and its consequences for business competitiveness, have frequently failed to comment on a major difference between the Japanese and the Western approach to Total Quality.

Much of the current British and American interest in Total Quality has focused on the business and human aspects of the subject. People have concentrated on the importance of motivation for quality, organising quality circles, establishing the right sort of relationships with suppliers, and so on.

The importance of these matters should not be understated, and the previous two sections of the book have been concerned with them, but it would be foolish to ignore the fact that Japanese industry, by contrast, has built its reputation for quality on the solid foundation of technology, through the use of statistical quality control (SQC) and, in particular, of statistical process control (SPC).

The business and motivational issues are important, but they alone will not produce the continuously improving quality which is characteristic of Japanese industry. To achieve this, you must understand and use the technological tools.

We will begin by clarifying some definitions. By SQC we mean the whole area of the application of the science of statistics to the control of quality. SQC provides a great many tools which can be applied to a large variety of quality problems. Some of the most important will be reviewed here and in Chapter 12. SPC is the part of SQC which is concerned with the monitoring and control of processes. It is particularly important in manufacturing, but can also be used in other areas.

PRINCIPAL ELEMENTS OF SPC

The normal distribution is at the root of statistical process control

At the root of SPC is the concept of *the normal distribution*. This has been mentioned already in Chapter 10, and most people have at least some knowledge of it, but it is probably wise at this point to offer a brief refresher summary of its main features.

The normal distribution is most easily explained by an example. We will take the simple mechanical engineering case of a lathe being used to turn small pins. The nominal diameter is 20mm, and the draughtsman has set a tolerance on it of $\pm 20\mu$m. However hard the turner tries to produce pins of exactly 20mm diameter, there will be small random variations caused by a multitude of factors connected with the accuracy of the machine, the sharpness of the cutting tool, the hardness of the metal from which the pins are cut, and the skill of the operator. If we take a batch of 50 pins and measure their diameters, we can classify them by diameter in steps of 2μm, and plot a histogram showing how many measure between 20 and 20.002mm, how many between 20.002 and 20.004mm, and so on.

Fig. 11.1 shows a typical histogram produced in this way. As you would expect, most of the pins come close to the target size of 20mm, and there are fewer pins with diameters further away from the target value. If we were to take a large number of pins and divide them into narrower size bands, we would begin to approximate to a curve such as that shown in Fig. 11.2. This is called a normal distribution, and it is found wherever quantities vary in a random fashion. You will get a similar curve by weighing a large number of eggs, measuring the height of a large number of adult men, or even counting the number of cornflakes in packets of the same nominal weight (if you have the time to spare!). If the variations really are

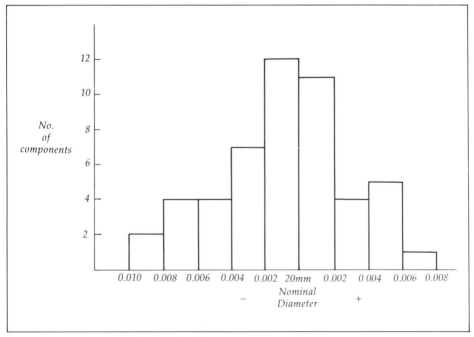

Fig. 11.1. Diameters of a sample of 50 pins

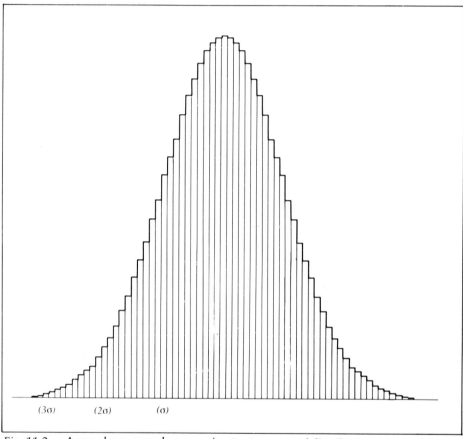

Fig. 11.2.   A very large sample approximates to a normal distribution

random, and are just as likely to be upwards as downwards from the central value, the curve will be symmetrical and will always have the same shape, though particular versions of it may appear to be flattened or squeezed up.

Standard deviation tells you how well a process can perform in relation to a tolerance

This curve has some very special properties. For one thing, it can be completely defined by just two numbers: the mean, which is the central value, and a quantity known as *the standard deviation*, which is a measure of the scatter of values on either side of the mean. There is a simple formula for calculating this, and every scientific pocket calculator has a button which will work it out for you automatically.

If you mark off a distance equal to the standard deviation on either side of the mean, as in Fig. 11.3, the area under the curve contained between these two lines is just over 68% of the total area under the curve. That means 68% of items in a large random sample will fall within one standard deviation of the mean. Statisticians always use the Greek letter sigma (σ) to represent the standard deviation. More than 95% of the sample will fall between the limits of twice the standard deviation on either side of the mean, and virtually all the sample – 99.8% – will be contained within the area of three standard deviations. The shaded area between any two limits represents the probability of a component lying between them (Fig. 11.4).

The curve shows the level of consistency which it is possible to maintain with the process running as it is. No matter what the tolerance written on the drawing may be, all you can expect is that virtually all the parts you produce will be within a range of six times the standard deviation. This gives an indication of what is called the *process capability* of the operation.

The curve also tells you how well you are doing in relation to your specified tolerance. If the mean is halfway

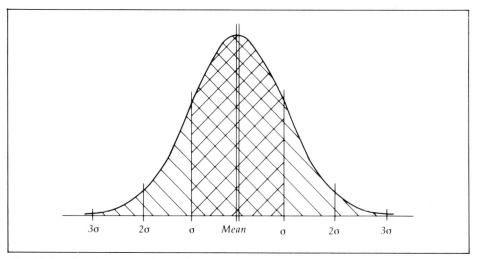

Fig. 11.3.   In a large sample, 68% of items will be within ± σ, 95% within ± 2σ

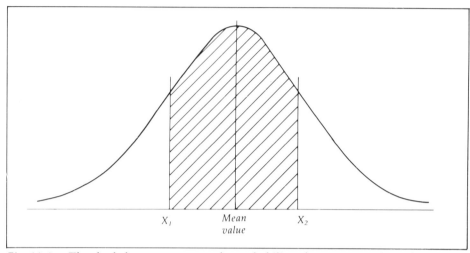

Fig. 11.4.   The shaded area represents the probability of a component lying between X_1 and X_2

between the two limits and the 2σ lines come inside the limits, then more than 95% of the pins are within the tolerance limits. If the mean has drifted to one side, or the tolerance limits have been set more tightly, you will have a proportion of out-of-tolerance work, which is given by the area of the curve outside the tolerance limits. So the standard deviation can tell you how realistic the tolerance is for the process you are running.

There are several definitions of process capability which show the relationship between the drawing tolerance and the achievable performance. Under one definition you divide the tolerance range by the standard deviation. In our example, with a tolerance of $\pm$ 20μm, if the standard deviation is 3μm, the process capability is 20/3, or 6.7 standard deviations. This means the tolerance limits would be a little outside the 3σ marks on either side and that therefore the process is barely capable: any drift of the mean, and the machine will start to produce defective parts. Much more healthy would be a process capability of 8σ or more. If it is down to 4σ or less , the process needs to be improved.

A slightly different definition of process capability is

used by the Ford Motor Company in its SPC manual. This takes into account the fact that it may be difficult in some processes to keep the process mean in the middle of the tolerance band, so whichever is the shorter distance is divided by σ to obtain the process capability (Fig. 11.5).

You may have noticed that a little 'cheating' has been going on in the last few paragraphs. We started by talking about a batch of 50 pins, then went on to describe the curve which would be approximated by a large number of pins, and finally listed some properties of that curve. How does that curve relate to our original sample of 50?

Samples can tell you a lot about the population they belong to

To deal with that question, the relationship between samples and what is called the 'population' of which they are a part must be examined. Suppose that, instead of making 50 pins one after another and then measuring

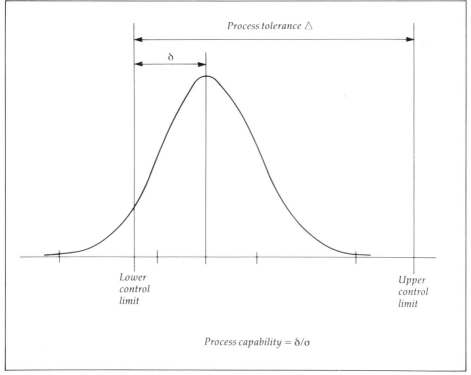

Fig. 11.5   Ford Motor Company's definition of process capability

them, we take a sample of 50 at random out of a bin containing a large population of pins, all nominally of the same size. The mean and standard deviation of the contents of the bin are not known – we would have to measure every pin to find out – but we can estimate it from the mean and standard deviation of our sample. We can even put a figure on the probability that we shall be correct.

All this is true for large samples. What is particularly important for our purposes is that it is also approximately true for quite small samples. The mathematical rules are rather different, but that need not concern us here. The difficult calculations have all been done and can be looked up in tables, and when dealing with small samples we can simplify things further by working with the range (the difference between the largest and the smallest item in a sample) instead of the standard deviation.

SPC AND QUALITY CONTROL

Sampling inspection implies that you are prepared to accept some defectives

There are two important but quite different ways in which this information about normal distributions and samples can be used to help control quality. The first and perhaps less important of the two techniques is sampling inspection. A typical example is if you have a large consignment of 10,000 widgets which has just been delivered from a supplier, and you want to know if they are good. It would be too expensive to inspect every one, so you must find some other way of making an assessment.

The essential point to remember about sampling inspection is that it involves a risk. If you are not prepared to accept any defective products at all – perhaps because they are critically important for safety – then there is no point in carrying out sampling inspection. You must either trust your supplier, or carry out 100% inspection. Even 100% inspection is not 100% reliable, and some companies will inspect a batch twice if the products are safety-critical.

The idea of accepting defective work runs counter to all we have been saying about Total Quality, and this is why companies which have committed themselves to Total

Quality are very careful in their use of sampling inspection. They will employ it only to check new suppliers until confidence in them is established, and as an occasional spot-check on established suppliers. They do not use it for regular inspection.

To return to the batch of 10,000 widgets. You will know for certain that not every widget will be absolutely identical, and it is possible that some will be outside the acceptable limits. What you would like to do is to take a sample from the batch, and from the quality of the sample to get a reliable estimate of the scatter of widgets in the whole batch. This will tell you whether the process is controlled to within your specification limits.

The complicated arithmetic involved in this task is readily available: there are sets of standard tables you can refer to. These operate in different ways, but they will require details such as what percentage of defective widgets you are prepared to tolerate in the whole batch, and how certain you need to be that the answer is correct. There are two aspects to this uncertainty: there is the chance that you will accept a batch which is worse than you are prepared to tolerate, and the chance that you will reject a batch which is not as bad as it appears to be from the sample.

With this information, the tables will tell you how big a sample you will have to take, and whether to reject the whole batch if you find one or more defective parts in the sample. If you perform sampling inspection you must adhere to the rules. If the tables tell you to reject the batch, you must either return the whole batch to your supplier, if that is the contract you have with him or her, or you must sort the whole batch.

There are various refinements to sampling plans, but they are not widely used. There are plans in which you can go on taking a series of samples until you are sufficiently confident to accept or reject the batch. There are plans which, instead of asking whether items are acceptable or unacceptable (sampling by attributes), are based on measurement of a dimension (sampling by variables). Plans of this sort can reach a high level of precision, but if you need that degree of certainty you will probably do better to insist that your supplier uses statistical process control.

SPC, unlike sampling, prevents the production of bad work

Sampling plans are used to trap defective work after it has been produced, so they are an appraisal technique. More important for Total Quality is statistical process control (SPC), which is a technique aimed at preventing the production of bad work. Earlier in this book we talked about assignable causes and random variations, and said that the assignable causes must be identifed and eliminated and the random variations then controlled. SPC concerns the control of random variations. It relies on the normal distribution, which, as has been shown describes the random variations in a process. If you have not eliminated the assignable causes of errors, your process will not conform to a normal distribution and you cannot use SPC.

As with sampling plans, SPC relies on the fact that there is a connection between the characteristics of a sample – its mean and its standard deviation or range – and the characteristics of the whole population from which it has been drawn. The principal tool of SPC is the control chart, and to explain one way of constructing and using it we will return to the example of the 20mm turned pins.

When he or she is confident that the operation is running satisfactorily, the operator takes a sample of, say, five pins and measures their diameters. He or she adds together the diameters and divides by five to obtain their mean diameter, and then takes the difference between the largest and the smallest diameter in the sample as the range. After some time he or she takes a second sample and finds its mean and range, which will probably be slightly different from the first sample. This is repeated several times until there are about ten samples, and he or she is now in a position to create control charts.

First, he or she calculates the population mean from all the samples and takes this as the central reference line (Fig. 11.6). Then he or she calculates the mean value of all the ranges of the samples to obtain an average range. Because there is a connection between the scatter of measurements in a sample and the scatter in the whole population, he or she is now able to multiply the mean range by a constant,

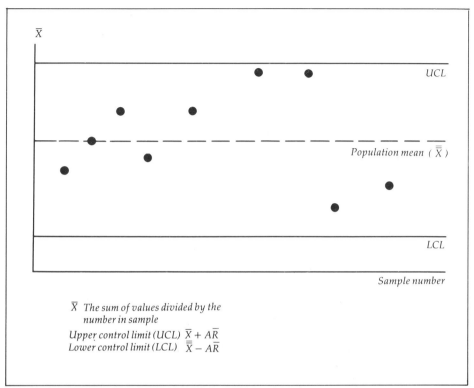

$\overline{X}$

UCL

Population mean ($\overline{\overline{X}}$)

LCL

Sample number

$\overline{X}$ *The sum of values divided by the
number in sample*

*Upper control limit (UCL) $\overline{\overline{X}} + A\overline{R}$
Lower control limit (LCL) $\overline{\overline{X}} - A\overline{R}$*

Fig. 11.6. Control chart for means

which depends on the size of the sample, to obtain the position of the 'control limits' above and below the mean (Fig. 11.6).

These control limits correspond to the position of the 3σ lines Fig. 11.3, so that as long as the process continues at the same level of reliability, 99.7% of future samples taken should have their average between these two limits. From now on, the operator is able to chart the progress of his or her work by taking samples periodically and plotting the mean value on the chart, which is usually called an 'X-bar' chart because X is the symbol used by statisticians to represent the mean. He or she may also create another chart such as that shown in Fig. 11.7, called an 'R' chart, because R stands for the range. On this he or she plots the range of each sample, and there is a control limit,

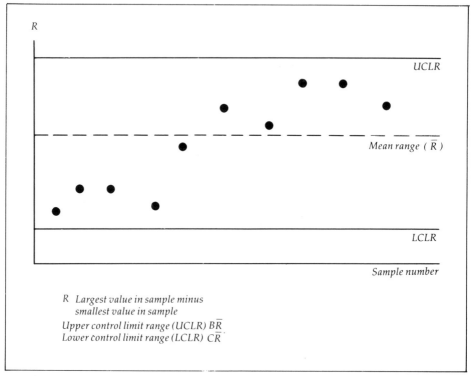

Fig. 11.7.   Control chart for ranges

calculated in the same way as for the X chart, indicating the limit beyond which the range should not increase.

Control chart limits are not the same as drawing tolerances   It should be noted that nothing has been said as yet about the drawing tolerance. The control limits on the X chart have nothing to do with the tolerance: they simply show the capability of the process. If the tolerance limits are comfortably wider than the control limits, then you have a process which is capable. A process may be under control – that is, it conforms to the normal distribution – but yet not capable. If the tolerance limits fall inside the control limits, there is a problem: you cannot produce work which is consistently within tolerance, and will have to remove defective work by inspection, or take steps to improve the process.

The X and R charts are powerful weapons for controlling

a process. As long as each sample mean stays well inside the control limits, you know that the process is under control, and there will be no need to carry out 100% inspection.

Processes can be corrected before they go out of control

It is also possible to detect in good time if a process is tending to drift out of control, because the sample means will tend to move towards one of the control limits. In a machining operation, this could indicate tool wear which will require an adjustment to the machine or replacement of a tool. Whatever it is, the trend can be corrected before it leads to the production of defective work.

At the same time, the control chart also provides a safeguard against over-reacting to a trend. If a process is adjusted too soon and by too much, the next sample may breach the opposite control limit, so the operator or setter quickly learns to make the minimum adjustment necessary to keep the process under control.

The range chart is not used as regularly as the mean chart. With a new process it is often used for a short time to verify that the range does not vary greatly. It can be useful in operations where there is manual involvement as an indicator of fatigue, showing that the operator is beginning to lose control of the process. Because the operator is part of the control loop, it enables him or her to see what is happening and thus assists in bringing the process back under control. In an automatic process, an increase in the range points to a factor such as a fixture coming loose, a loss of hydraulic power, increased wear of bearings or suchlike. But in a reliable automatic process, it is often unnecessary to maintain a range chart.

CONTROL OF NON-MEASURABLE ATTRIBUTES

So far we have discussed control charts for variables. The variable may be a dimension, a voltage, a weight, a surface roughness, a hardness measurement: anything which can be measured on a continuous scale. However there are many characteristics which need to be controlled but which cannot be measured in this way. These may be either acceptable or unacceptable: only a curate's egg can be 'good in parts', and if a polished surface is scratched it is probably unacceptable. Such characteristics may have to be assessed subjectively – whether a cake is properly baked, for example.

In such cases, a method of control charting by attributes can be used, which is rather simpler than charting by variables. This is no excuse, though, for using methods such as go/not-go gauges instead of measuring dimensions. To use such a gauge is to throw away the opportunity to control a process, because you do not know what is happening to the process until it has gone out of control. Sampling by attributes is often suitable in the food and other process industries where items are inspected visually as they are manufactured, and either accepted or rejected.

Sometimes an intermediate kind of measurement is possible. For example, the number of flaws in the surface of castings could be counted, or the number of scratches or blemishes on paintwork, and the information used in a control chart for 'variables'. This method has to be used with caution, because there is no optimum number of such defects – the desired figure is zero – so that a lower control limit is something of an oddity. It can be useful, though, because if several batches in a row fall below the lower control limit, there is a good reason for studying the process to discover the reason and perhaps to improve the general level of quality.

Attribute sampling like this can be applied effectively in non-manufacturing areas, for example in monitoring the number of customer complaints in an airline or a hotel. Another application might be for measuring the time taken by a switchboard operator to answer telephone calls. The main use for control charting in situations like these is to check whether performance is getting better or worse. It is particularly helpful during improvement projects, in providing a reliable and impartial check on the effectiveness of any changes that have been introduced; it will show whether they have made any difference, and whether that difference represents an improvement.

ADVANTAGES AND POTENTIAL PITFALLS OF SPC

SPC fuels a policy of continuous improvement

SPC is a valuable technique because it helps and encourages you to make continual improvements to your processes. If your control limits are well within specification limits, you know that you can reduce the level of inspection and hence your prevention costs, while assuring your customer of a high-quality product. If the control limits are too wide, SPC provides a tool for experimentation, enabling you to see the effects on the process of any improvements you make to it.

As manufacturing variance is reduced with the help of SPC, there is an important consequence for your measuring equipment. The factor that determines how accurate a measuring instrument must be is not the design tolerance, but the SPC control limit. Your measuring capability must be well inside the process capability of the production machine. It follows, therefore, that the more closely you succeed in controlling the process, the more accurate the measuring equipment must be.

SPC has been around for a long time. The first British Standard on control charts was published in 1935, and the theory was developed even earlier by Professor R. A. Fisher, but it has been used only spasmodically by British industry, and mostly in defence applications. In the USA it was taken up by W. A. Shewhart and W. E. Deming, but received equally lukewarm attention. It was not until after the Second World War, when Dr Deming took the ideas to Japan, where they were adopted enthusiastically, that British and US industry really woke up to the value of SPC.

SPC can be used in small batch manufacture

There are possibly two reasons for this delay, one of which could be particularly relevant to the British scene. As outlined earlier, the control chart is something which requires the user to take samples adding up to at least 50 pieces before he or she can even construct the chart, and it is only then that he or she begins to reap the benefit from it. A large proportion of the British engineering industry manufactures its products in batches of 50 or less, so it is not even possible to get to the point of creating a reliable control chart.

However, there is a way in which control charts can be used to good effect even in small batch manufacture. With this method, instead of trying to control the accuracy of each individual batch, the aim is to monitor and improve the machine or process which is being used to manufacture the work – even when batch quantities are down to one.

For instance, if you have a group of lathes which are being used regularly to turn work of between 150 and 200mm in diameter, you can find out how well they perform the job. You will get the most reliable results if you can restrict the machines to one type. Take samples of 30 or more pieces turned within the size range, and find the difference between each actual value and its target value. In this way you get a measure of the dispersion, without being tied to a single diameter. From this you can calculate a standard deviation, just as you can with samples taken from a single nominal diameter. It will probably not give enough information to allow the creation of a proper control chart, but it will enable you to compare the tolerances which you are supposed to be achieving with the standard deviation that you are actually getting.

In one such exercise carried out on the machining centres in a major flexible manufacturing system (FMS), it was found that the standard deviation was equal to the design tolerance. This meant that 30% of the work could always be expected to be out of tolerance, so that 100% inspection of the work was obligatory. In addition, because multiple dimensions were machined on the workpieces, it meant that rectification work had to be done on virtually 100% of the work.

Statistical process capability monitoring will show deteriorating trends in plant

Since it monitors the capability of the process, this method can be used for one-off manufacturing, and is the only way in which monitoring can be performed in an FMS. When used as a long-term monitoring device, it can show if a machine is starting to deteriorate. It also provides useful information which can be sent to the design department, so that designers know what tolerances can realistically be applied to work going into the factory.

Many FMS and cells are not producing one-off work, but are turning out quite a small number of different components repetitively, though perhaps in random sequence. In this situation a coordinate measuring machine can usefully be applied to carry out SPC, and special software packages are available to perform this task automatically.

Computer aids bring dangers as well as benefits

The other possible reason for the slow adoption of SPC may be that it has been presented in too technical and specialised a language, giving the impression that it was difficult to apply. It is possible that the introduction of computer aids to SPC is persuading more companies to embark on it. A word of warning is needed, however. One industrial manager was recently heard to say that he couldn't implement SPC because he did not have the software for his computer. He perhaps did not appreciate that all you need to do SPC is a pencil and a piece of graph paper.

There is also a danger that computer aids will lead people to imagine that they do not need to learn the fundamental principles of SPC. A computer will carry out complicated calculations very quickly, but unless you fully understand the significance of the figures that are being generated you can come to some extremely misleading conclusions. Computers are no substitute for a thorough training in the fundamentals of SPC.

Yet another danger is that computer-aided SPC will be misapplied. The whole purpose of SPC is to shorten the control loop: to enable the operator at the machine to improve a process. If the result of computer analysis is fed straight back to him or her, it can save time and effort and assist him or her in controlling the process. If, on the other hand, the information from several machines is networked into a central computer in the inspection department, and only made available to the operator via an inspector who goes and tells him or her what is wrong, the control loop is lengthened or even destroyed, and the operator may also lose the motivation to keep the process under control.

ACTION SUMMARY

- Does anyone in your organisation have a good grasp of statistical methods?
- What are the capabilities of your key processes?
- Do you produce and use control charts?
- Do you use statistically valid sampling plans?

If the answers do not accord well with the method outline in this chapter, then:

- Run an education programme in statistical methods. Start at the top. You cannot manage the use of statistical methods without some understanding.
- Measure the process capabilities on key products and processes.
- Improve the processes until they have at least 6σ capability.
- Implement control charts.
- Continue improving the processes.

12 ADVANCED METHODS OF QUALITY CONTROL

To conclude this section on the technology which underpins Total Quality, we will briefly review some of the more advanced aids which can be brought to bear in reducing product variability. In Chapter 6 we described some of the techniques such as brainstorming and Pareto analysis which can be used by quality improvement groups after a small amount of training. Some companies also introduce SPC and control charts by initially teaching them to their more experienced quality improvement groups. The techniques described in this chapter, though, are more appropriately used by specialist technicians or professional engineers, because they not only involve more advanced mathematics but also require a deeper understanding of the capabilities and limitations of statistical methods.

VARIATION RESEARCH TECHNIQUE

Variation research offers a succession of techniques for dealing with problem processes

These problem-solving methods are often grouped together under the name Variation Research Technique (VRT) not because they have much in common, but because they form a succession of increasingly powerful procedures for dealing with processes which are causing problems. Some of the most important of these methods are listed in Fig. 12.1. It is only necessary to turn to such more complex techniques when a serious problem is encountered which does not respond to the simpler methods such as brainstorming or Pareto analysis.

When you believe you have found and dealt with the root cause or causes of a particular problem, it is good practice to go through an exercise called 'turn off and on', which means that you remove what you believe has cured the problem to see if the trouble returns. For example, if you believe you have tracked down the cause of

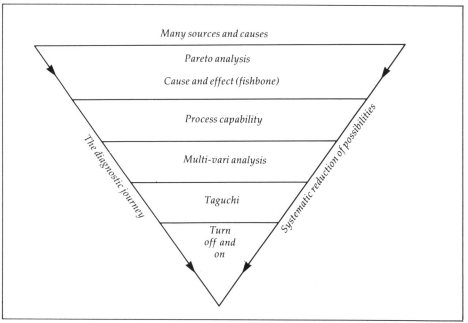

Fig. 12.1.   *Variation Research Technique – VRT – provides increasingly powerful procedures*

irregularity in size of some workpieces to temperature variation in the coolant system of the machine tool, and have installed a refrigeration system which appears to have cured the problem, you should then try turning off the refrigeration system to see if the trouble returns.

Strictly speaking this step is necessary (and it is certainly possible to be mistaken in thinking you have found a cure, when in fact totally different factors have been at work). But it requires considerable discipline to carry out a 'turn off and on' exercise, and most managers will simply keep a sharp eye on the process to make sure the trouble does not recur. If it does, then further steps will have to be taken.

MULTI-VARI ANALYSIS

Use multi-vari analysis where several factors may be at work

The first technique which starts to go beyond the capability of most shop-floor quality improvement groups is multi-vari analysis. This is a development of SPC which can be enlisted in cases where several factors may be influencing the result of a process and it is difficult to identify which are the most important elements to be controlled. You could try varying them one at a time to see what happens, but this can take a long time. More importantly, some factors may influence each other.

Multi-vari study divides the possible causes of variation under three headings:

- Within-piece variation.
- Piece-to-piece variation.
- Time-to-time variation.

Study of *within-piece variation* will reveal what is being produced consistently wrongly all the time, for example, an unwanted taper on a shaft, or a badly covered area in spray-painted components. *Piece-to-piece variation* might result from irregularities in the hardness of material being worked, or faulty fixturing. *Time-to-time variation* could result for example from tool wear, temperature variations, or change of operators.

Analysing production data in this way may reveal that

the piece-to-piece variability is small, but that there is large variation over a period of time. So it helps to narrow down the area within which you must search to find the main cause or causes of trouble. Examples of multi-vari analyses in which within-piece, piece-to-piece and time-to-time variations, respectively, were revealed as the main source of variation are shown in Figs. 12.2 (a), (b), and (c).

One highly rewarding example of multi-vari analysis was in a machine shop where the plant manager had decided, on the basis of a process capability study, that a turret lathe was not accurate enough for the work it was required to do, and the manager was therefore on the point of ordering a new machine tool. Fig. 12.3 shows the result of a multi-vari analysis performed on the problem. Measurements were taken of two diameters to find the out-of-roundness at both ends of the shaft, on three successive shafts. This was repeated at hourly intervals over five hours. Fig. 12.4 is an explanation of the results plotted in Fig. 12.3. Out-of-roundness is shown by the vertical height of each black lozenge shape, and taper by the slope from left to right of the lozenge (Fig. 12.3). Piece-to-piece variation is shown by the difference between pieces in the sample taken at one time, and time-to-time variation is indicated by variations right across the chart.

The study revealed that the lathe was producing some out-of-roundness at one end of the shaft, and that there was a negligible amount of taper, but that within each piece the variation was well within the required tolerance. It also showed that between successive pieces the variation was not sufficient to cause difficulty.

The most significant variations were those which appeared over a longer time. Looking more closely at the possible causes of such variations uncovered a few simple things which made a substantial difference, such as that the coolant reservoir was not being topped up frequently enough and that coolant temperatures fluctuated widely.

The machine itself was found to be well within the process capability, although there were minor problems of out-of-roundness and taper which were dealt with by straightforward maintenance work and checking on feeds

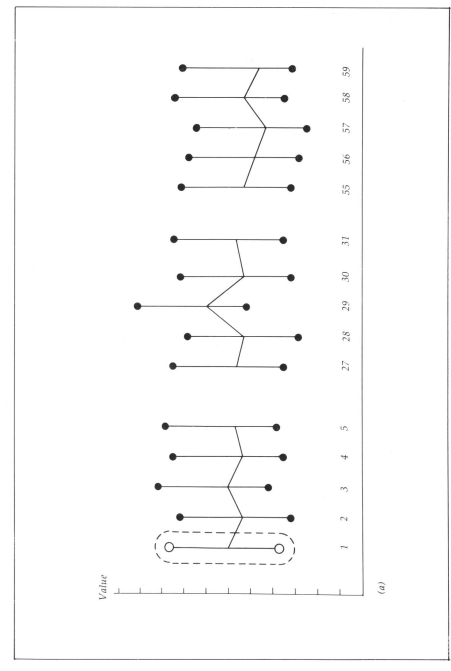

Fig. 12.2. Analysis of (a) within-piece, (b) piece-to-piece, and (c) time-to-time variations reveals the largest source of variations

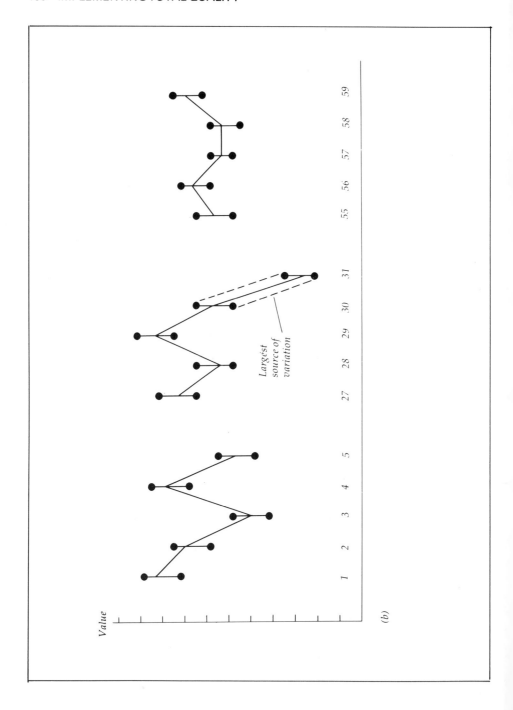

(b)

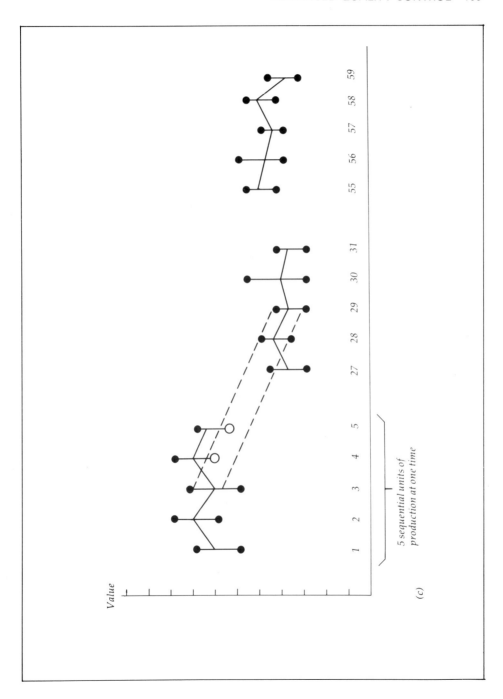

Value

5 *sequential units of*
production at one time

(c)

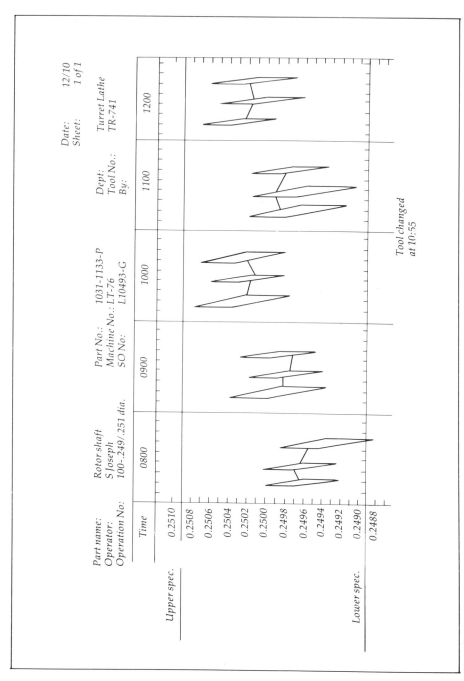

Fig. 12.3.   Multi-vari analysis of rotor shaft produced on a turret lathe

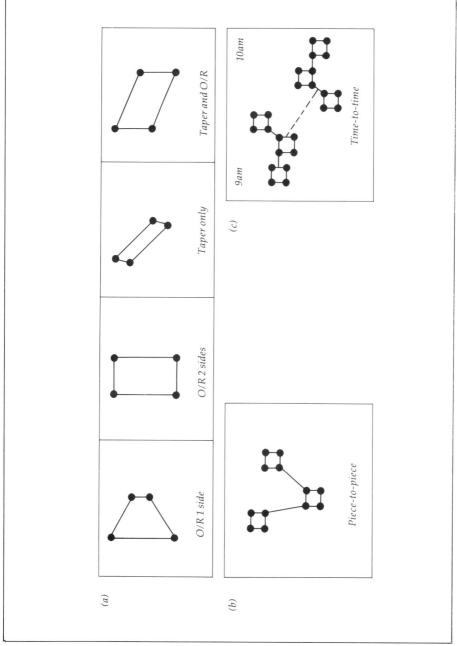

Fig. 12.4. Explanation of the multi-vari data in Fig. 12.3: (a) within-piece, (b) piece-to-piece, and (c) time-to-time

and speeds. The works director than had a ritual tearing-up of the order for a new machine.

TAGUCHI METHODS

In the case just cited, the number of factors which might contribute to the problem was small, and there was no serious interaction between them. As factors multiply and the likelihood of interactions increases, a more formalised method of experimentation has to be adopted to avoid jumping to wrong conclusions.

Taguchi methods allow study of many variables with only a few trials

The theory of design of experiments dates back to the 1920s and the work of R. A. Fisher, who developed it originally for agricultural research. Its use in industrial applications owes most of its popularity to the Japanese statistician Genichi Taguchi, whom we mentioned in Chapter 8. Taguchi developed orthogonal array designs to support his work in helping to rebuild the Japanese telephone system after the Second World War. He provided a set of techniques which allow examination of a complex process with many variables, and which permit, in a relatively restricted number of trials, the identification of the main control factors and their optimum levels.

Taguchi methods have been applied extensively to the design of both products and processes. The basic principle is the same in both cases, and it stands the classical approach to quality on its head. Instead of trying to identify and eliminate the causes of quality problems, Taguchi methods seek to design a product or process which is insensitive to the causes. The idea is to eliminate the effect instead of trying to remove the cause.

The problem with conducting experiments in an industrial situation is that there are many factors which can affect the desired output. Even a fairly simple process may involve ten or more factors which can influence the quality of the product. To study all possible combinations of ten factors at only two levels, each would involve 2^{10} or 1,024 experiments – not counting any repetition to prove the accuracy of the result.

Taguchi uses the properties of orthogonal matrices to produce experimental designs which require far fewer experiments. For example, it is possible to set up a design to study the effect of 15 different input factors with only 16 experiments. There are standard designs available for different numbers of factors at either two or three levels of each factor. It is in fact possible to manipulate the designs to examine an individual factor at almost any number of levels.

These techniques are best explained by a simple example. An industrial cleaning process involved washing glass with a solution of methanol and sodium hydroxide in water. Variable factors which were thought to influence the process included the concentration of the solution, the temperature, the washing time and whether the glass was brushed or just rinsed. A system for measuring the cleanliness of the surface was devised, based on the attenuation of transmitted light.

Only five factors were involved, but the experiment used what is known as an L8 design, capable of addressing seven separate factors. This meant that eight individual experiments were required. Fig. 12.5 shows the design. Each factor is studied at two levels, which are represented by either '1' or '2' in the matrix. The concentration of sodium hydroxide at Level 1 is zero, and at Level 2 is 10%. Each row of the matrix represents a single experiment, with the levels of the factors identified by a 1 or a 2 in the relevant column.

It can be seen from Fig. 12.5 that there are four experiments with the concentration of sodium hydroxide equal to zero, and four with 10% sodium hydroxide. The other factors are randomly distributed among these two sets of four experiments, so that their effects cancel out. We can therefore compare the average level of cleanliness resulting from the two different concentrations.

The important point to note is that although we have only carried out eight experiments in total, we have four repetitions of our experiment for each factor. By contrast, to have done this for all possible combinations would have involved 128 experiments.

	Factor						
	A	B	C	D	E	e	e
Experiment							
1	1	1	1	1	1	1	1
2	1	1	1	2	2	2	2
3	1	2	2	1	1	2	2
4	1	2	2	2	2	1	1
5	2	1	2	1	2	1	2
6	2	1	2	2	1	2	1
7	2	2	1	1	2	2	1
8	2	2	1	2	1	1	2

Factor	Description	Level 1	Level 2
A	Sodium hydroxide	0%	10%
B	Methanol	0%	20%
C	Temperature	25C	50C
D	Time	15sec	35sec
E	Brushing	With	Without

Example: Experiment number 7 has Sodium hydroxide 10%
Methanol 20%
Temperature 25C
Time 15 seconds
Brushing without

Fig. 12.5.   Taguchi experiment design for an industrial cleaning process

ANOVA techniques establish the most important causes of variation

Once the experimental results have been obtained, they can be analysed using analysis of variance (ANOVA) techniques to establish which are the most important factors. The variation resulting from each factor is compared against experimental error. The two columns headed 'e' in Fig. 12.5 are used to assist in the estimation of experimental error. Among other things this particular experiment demonstrated that the best solution for cleaning was plain water.

Similar experiments have been conducted to optimise mechanical and electronic product designs. One example was the design of the door-hinge for a motor car. The quality characteristics required were a uniform effort in opening the door, and the absence of noise. In this case 13 factors covering the design of the spring and the geometry of the hinge were used. Use of Taguchi methods identified three of the 13 characteristics as being critical to performance. This led to significant cost savings by reducing the amount of attention required on the other ten factors.

Product design, as described by Taguchi, takes place in three stages. First comes *system design*, which involves innovation and specialist knowledge of the technologies appropriate to the work of the designer, whether it concerns a door-hinge or an electronic circuit. It is this aspect of design which ensures that the product will function.

The next stage he calls *parameter design*. In an electronic circuit, for example, each parameter such as a resistor or a capacitor may be able to vary by quite a large amount and still meet the requirement of the circuit. Similarly with a door-hinge, where the designer has considerable discretion over the levels at which the parameters are set.

The functioning of a product is influenced by controllable factors and by uncontrollable 'noise' factors

What Taguchi is effectively asserting is that there are two classes of factors which have an impact on the manufacture and functioning of a product. There are controllable factors, such as the design levels of resistors and capacitors, or the dimensions of a hinge, and there are also uncontrollable factors – what Taguchi calls 'noise factors' – inherent in the variability of the components or the manufacturing process used. Parameter design aims at selecting the controllable factors in a design in such a way that they make the least demands on the uncontrollable noise factors. This means, for example, designing an electronic circuit so that it will function satisfactorily using the lowest-cost components supplied to wide tolerance specifications.

The third stage of design is *tolerance design*. This is only required if the efforts of parameter design cannot produce the required performance without special components or high process accuracy. It involves tightening the tolerances on parameters where their variations can have a large influence on the final product.

Parameter design is a way of winning high quality at low cost

Most engineers in the USA and Europe overlook parameter design. They are conditioned to spend money to achieve product performance, rather than to find ways of modifying the design to gain high quality at low cost. Fig. 12.6 provides a highly illuminating contrast between the design approaches of US and Japanese engineers. It is safe to assume that British design practice is much closer to the American than to the Japanese model.

Taguchi focuses attention on the interactions between controllable and 'noise' factors in a design. His method involves calculating a 'signal-to-noise ratio', (analogous to the function of the same name in signal processing), and selecting the design parameters to make the signal-to-noise ratio as high as possible. This is done by use of orthogonal matrices similar to those we have already discussed.

The great advantage of this approach is that correct choice of parameters results in wider tolerances. Users of the technique speak of increasing the signal-to-noise ratio – cutting the variability – in electronic circuits by 800%, while using very low-cost components. A Japanese manufacturer of ceramic tiles found that he was able to cut his percentage defective produced in a new kiln from 30% to less than 1% as a result of analysis using signal-to-noise ratio.

Another area where the technique is showing considerable promise is in the design of door closures in

Product system	USA	JAPAN
System	80%	40%
Parameter	2%	40%
Tolerance	18%	20%

Fig. 12.6.   Percentage of time spent on each of the three elements of design optimisation in the USA and in Japan

automobile bodies, something which has been a vexed question for many years. It is difficult to design a door closure which will operate smoothly in every case, because of all the variations during manufacture resulting from pressings which do not hold close tolerances for a variety of reasons; distortions and other errors introduced in welding of the pressings; further errors in the drilling of screw holes; and so on. Some factors can be controlled in the design of the body, the door, the hinges, the door seal, etc. On the other hand 'noise' can be introduced by variations in hardness of the sheet metal used in the pressings, by variations in the trimming of the pressings, by varying thermal distortions caused during welding, by differences between weld fixtures, and by other factors.

Taguchi techniques are powerful, but require professional treatment

Taguchi's technique involves building a test matrix based on the various controllable factors, which is called an 'inner array', and superimposing on it another matrix based on the principal noise factors, called the 'outer array'. For test purposes the 'uncontrollable' noise factors are artificially controlled, so that if a voltage, a temperature or a dimension is prone to vary in an uncontrolled way during normal production, it is actually set in the test sampling, generally at a typical level and at a 'worst case' level. A data matrix is then produced in which test results are obtained for different combinations of controllable and uncontrollable factors.

From the results of this testing, it is possible to plot the way the signal-to-noise ratio varies with changes in each of the controllable factors, as well as the influence of controllable factors on the performance of the equipment; and from the combined information, the optimum values can be set for the controllable factors.

This approach offers a way of dealing with large amounts of variability. It brings complicated design problems within the scope of ANOVA techniques. Software that will work through data of this kind quickly and easily is now available for use with personal computers. As with SPC, if you do not fully understand the mathematical basis of this type of analysis, you can be misled by the ease of computer methods, and make some expensive mistakes in decisions about costly processes or plant investments. Handling such analyses, even though computers have removed most of the laborious calculations, requires the expertise of a professional engineer trained in this type of statistical work.

Design of experiments, and the Taguchi method in particular, is the most powerful tool available for reducing manufacturing variance, once full benefit has been derived from conventional techniques. The significance which is placed on this method by Japanese industry is clearly shown in Fig. 12.7, which envisages about 80% of the

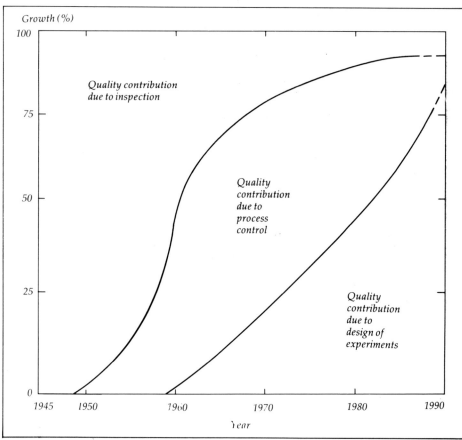

Fig. 12.7.   Expected growth in importance to Total Quality of design of experiments in Japanese industry

contribution to quality coming from design of experiments by 1990. Small wonder, then, that there is rapidly growing interest in Taguchi methods on both sides of the Atlantic.

ACTION SUMMARY

- Is your process capability better than 8o?
- What benefits could you obtain from reduced manufacturing variance in terms of improved customer satisfaction, better product performance and lower costs?

If the answer to the first question is 'no' and that to the second question is 'significant', then:

- Run a management education programme in VRT (especially in Taguchi methods).
- Identify pilot projects for improvement.
- Train specialists.
- Set up task groups with specialists and line staff to work on pilot projects.
- Spread the techniques throughout the organisation.

IMPLEMENTATION

We have shown you what Total Quality has done for many companies and what it can do for yours. All that remains, if we have succeeded in convincing you, is to go ahead and put it into practice. The next chapter outlines the implementation programme step by step, and enclosed with this book is a flow chart which may be helpful as a display to put on your wall to keep a record of the state of progress of your implementation plan.

There are many other new quality techniques already in use in Japan which will, when adopted, have a significant effect on western manufacturing industry. Such techniques are beyond the scope of this book, but we hope in future to bring you news of them.

Total Quality is a vitally important strategy for today's business. It is practical, and every company can profit from it. Your competitors are probably implementing it now. If you think you are nearly there already, check carefully. You may be further from Total Quality than you think. If you decide you are still short of the goal of Total Quality (and it's a moving target) then start now.

13 THE IMPLEMENTATION PROCESS

In the course of this book we have examined the issues of Total Quality, starting with a description of the task and proceeding to discuss the people, systems and technologies involved. When Total Quality is introduced into an organisation, all these factors must be brought together, and an implementation that deals first with people, then with systems and then with technology, or some other such sequence, is not viable. This chapter describes how to start a Total Quality programme and bring it to a state where the process of continuous improvement is institutionalised.

The flow chart enclosed in this book shows the Total Quality implementation process. There are six main steps:

- Understanding.
- Top management commitment.
- Company-wide awareness.
- Planning.
- Implementation.
- Review (leading to increased understanding and continuous improvement).

Implementation is shown divided into the categories of people, technology and structure which we have used throughout this book. Each of these categories can be further subdivided, and in the chart, action in each of these categories and subdivisions is shown occurring concurrently. The time sequence of all this activity depends on the individual organisation and the opportunities to be gained from Total Quality.

UNDERSTANDING

The rustic story along the lines of 'if you want to go there I wouldn't start from here' has been told many times. The problem is that it is always necessary to start from 'here' but it is not always clear in an organisational sense, where 'here' is. The exercise of finding out is often referred to as a diagnostic, which is simply a structured examination of how well the organisation is suited to its tasks, in terms of its people, systems and technology.

In Total Quality there are a number of keys to diagnosis, and these have been discussed earlier in this book. If you have followed through some of the action points at the end of the relevant chapters, you will already have assimilated much of the information.

The first thing to examine is how your quality system compares to the standard BS5750. This is very much a basic set of rules. The fact that your organisation is certified to BS5750 does not mean that you are obtaining all the benefits possible from Total Quality. However, if there are major elements of the standard missing from your system, then you will need to put these in place before proceeding any further. It is important to ensure that your system is being applied thoroughly in practice, and is not just there to impress your customers or the British Standards Institute. An effective quality assurance system is the basis for Total Quality: 'a window dressing' system can make the entire Total Quality effort 'window dressing' too.

Once you have examined how well your system compares to BS5750, the next stage is to look at how far you are using statistics effectively. There is no national standard to advise you as to the best practice in this regard. There are, however, several British Standards on the technical issues of application. A good basis for evaluating your operations in this area is to obtain a copy of Ford's excellent Quality System Standard Q-101, and compare your operations to its requirements. This does not cover the use of SPC techniques in administrative areas, but if you are already applying these extensively you probably do not need to be reading this chapter.

The third part of this task of examining what stage you are at is to carry out an attitude and awareness survey, to find out how far your staff understand Total Quality. This should consist of no more than half-a-dozen questions, covering some of the key points in this book, e.g. 'what do you mean by quality?' and 'who is most responsible for quality in the organisation?'

This can either be done as a questionnaire, or as a series of brief interviews. If interviews are used, they should not take more than a quarter of an hour each, or you are going into too much detail. When we carry out these exercises we like to look at about 10% of employees, with the bias being towards management, but not excluding the shop-floor.

The final part of the 'understanding' exercise, and one of the most important, is the identification of your quality cost structure. In Chapter 8 we discussed the structure of quality costs, and the different uses to which they can be put. At the first stage of implementing Total Quality you should be looking closely at opportunities for quantifiable improvement. It is better to generate lower figures for potential savings which can be delivered than to come up with glittering opportunities which could only be realised on a greenfield site.

At the completion of this exercise you should know:

- How well your basic systems meet the task of ensuring product quality.
- How effectively you apply statistical methods.
- How aware your people are of quality.
- What opportunities you have for cost reduction through quality.

TOP MANAGEMENT COMMITMENT

Decision on the direction a company should take is the prerogative of senior management. Unless the board directs, there is no reason why anyone should follow, and without top management commitment any attempt to introduce Total Quality is a waste of time and effort.

Once the facts have been gathered, it is time to put them to the board and obtain that commitment. You can be sure you have such commitment if the board will submit to a three-day 'lock away' session on what Total Quality is and what it can do for their business. It is important to remember that this opportunity affects every business function, from sales to product development, and from purchasing to despatch. It is absolutely fundamental to the company's way of working. If the senior management will not take the time to understand it, then no one else is going to. On the other hand if the senior management will devote time to it, that in itself indicates the commitment required throughout the organisation.

The purpose of the three-day session is not just to educate, but also to devise a set of policy guidelines and an outline plan of action. The policy guidelines need to be concrete, but brief: about 20 points, covering not more than four sheets of paper should be the maximum. Policy statements saying nebulous things such as 'we will always supply good-quality products' can be unhelpful. Instead, the statements should include:

- A clear definition of quality.
- A commitment to meeting specifications every time.
- A commitment to continuing to reduce variance even when specifications are met.
- A statement on systems.
- A statement on training.

Other policy issues covered may include more general financial and personnel matters.

Once the policy statement is prepared, the next requirement is the outline plan of action. This should be aimed at taking the major opportunities exposed by the initial investigation. Action will be identified under the key areas of people, systems and technology, but only in general terms. For example, the board may commit itself to the introduction of SPC or Taguchi methods, or may want a quality circle programme, but the details of these programmes will not be worked out at this stage.

The proof that you have top management commitment is given when you establish a steering committee of senior functional managers chaired by the chief executive. The steering committee should then meet at least once a month, to provide direction and identify priorities. Eventually, Total Quality should be completely integrated into the business, and the function of the steering committee should be incorporated into regular board or management meetings. In the first stages of the programme of introducing Total Quality, however, it is important to have this clear identity. Otherwise it is too easy for the programme to be pushed further and further down the agenda every month until it slips into oblivion.

COMPANY-WIDE AWARENESS

Whatever the level of awareness shown by the preliminary study, there will be some need to explain Total Quality throughout the organisation. A top-to-bottom briefing exercise is often the best way to get this message across. It is essential to avoid mere sloganising and to emphasise the concrete nature of the activities and the objectives of improved competitiveness. The use of articles in company papers is also a good way of conveying the initial message, but again, it is important to avoid 'hype'. A typical briefing session should explain what quality is, why it is important, and what the company is going to do about it. This is likely to take about two hours. If it goes on for longer, there is probably too much detail.

At the completion of the awareness exercise it will be possible to measure the effect. This can be done by the simple expedient of repeating the earlier attitude survey. This is best done with a different 'sample' of staff from that used the first time, since the very fact that people have been surveyed increases their awareness of the issues in question. If there has been no clear effect, then there is something seriously wrong with the way in which the awareness exercise has been conducted.

PLANNING

Planning is 'what you do before you do anything so that you don't get mixed up when you do it'. From the initial outline plan, there will be a series of projects which have to be identified. These will cover education and training on a more extensive scale than the briefing programme, as well as the actions needed to realise the opportunities available. For each project, there should be a time-phased plan identifying targets and milestones, resources required, costs and projected benefits. The benefits should be reconciled with the original cost of quality estimates.

Once the plans are prepared, it is the task of the steering committee to prioritise them and to allocate resources. In our experience, it is a good idea to put into effect some projects which will show quick and clearly visible benefits early in the total programme. This helps to build up enthusiasm. Typical examples are in the SPC area, where the increased attention paid to processes by operators using SPC can in itself provide big savings. In one instance, we saw scrap rates on an automotive component fall from 10% to 0.1%, with the main factor being improved operator concentration.

IMPLEMENTATION

You are now at the point of executing your plans. There are certain key points to remember:

- Total Quality is not a 'once and for all' exercise. Improvement has to be built into the system.
- Total Quality begins and ends with education. It is not possible to do too much of this.
- Total Quality is about business improvement. Benefits should be quantified and reported. In this way senior management commitment is maintained.

In order to build Total Quality into a continuous improvement process, each functional manager should have quality objectives that are set annually. These objectives should be set cooperatively, in the same way that any other management objectives should be set. Realistic quality objectives will require planning for their achievement, and plans will require resources for their execution. Resource allocation must in turn be justified against the improvements demanded by the objectives. These individual plans taken together form a Total Quality improvement plan for the whole organisation. It is then up to the board to decide on priorities and to allocate resources. In this way, quality improvement becomes part of the corporate culture. The sequence is therefore:

- Agree objectives.
- Plan to meet the objectives.
- Identify resources to carry out the plans.
- Decide priorities.
- Allocate resources.
- Execute the plans.
- Review the results against the objectives.

Total Quality, as already stated, begins and ends with education. For implementation of each plan, there must be an element of both education and training: education in why the project is run, and training in the basic activities, procedures or skills necessary to carry out the tasks. It is almost impossible to overestimate the amount of education and training needed. In our experience 'overkill' always pays off in terms of smooth execution of the projects.

Total Quality concerns business improvement. Essentially this means increased profits. If Total Quality is to demonstrate benefits, the effect of reducing quality costs should be clearly shown. A reporting system will be needed which identifies quality costs on a regular basis. The system should be accurate, economical and timely. If the programme introducing Total Quality is geared towards producing early benefits, then the quality cost system needs to be set up early on in the programme to demonstrate the results as they come through.

The details of each individual project will be different. However, within any programme for implementing Total Quality, the subsequent process of continuous improvement projects will have a similar form. Almost invariably, we have found that it is best to start with a pilot exercise. This allows problems to be resolved on a small scale, and where the pilot project generates significant benefits, it generates enthusiasm which helps the full-scale implementation. The pilot follows these stages:

- Education in where the project fits into Total Quality and why it is happening.
- Training in the tasks that must be performed to make the project a success.
- Implementation of the pilot, with extensive support to follow up the training.
- Review of the results of the pilot against objectives.

In the light of the review, the project plan may be revised quite extensively before moving to the full-scale project. The full project then follows the same sequence of educate, train, implement and support, and final review.

REVIEW

As every project reaches completion it must be reviewed to see if the objectives have been achieved. In addition, because Total Quality is a continuous process, it is essential that the organisation's quality performance is regularly reviewed, using the form of diagnostic analysis which was described at the beginning of this chapter. The review will lead to increased understanding of the opportunities for further improvement. There will be a new set of issues for senior management to deal with. There will be a need for renewed commitment, fresh priorities and further resource allocations. The improvement process never stops, whether it involves a single process at shop-floor level, or the overall operation of a multinational business. The goal is always the same: improved operating performance through reduction of costs and elimination of waste, resulting in:

- Increased customer satisfaction.
- Increased sales.
- Higher profits.

FURTHER READING

Here is a short list of the most important publications currently in print which deal in greater depth with the topics covered in this book. There is as yet no satisfactory text book on the Taguchi approach to design of experiments.

BS5750: *A Positive Contribution to Better Business*. (For further details contact The British Standards Institution, 2 Park Street, London W1A 2BS.)

Feigenbaum, A.V., 1983. *Total Quality Control*. McGraw-Hill, New York.

Grant, E.L. and Leavenworth, R.S., 1980. *Statistical Quality Control*. McGraw-Hill, New York.

Juran, J.M. (Ed.), 1974. *Quality Control Handbook*. McGraw-Hill, New York.

Montgomery, D.C., 1984. *Design and Analysis of Experiments*. John Wiley & Sons, New York.